the emergence of memory

the emergence of memory

Conversations with W. G. SEBALD

Edited by LYNNE SHARON SCHWARTZ

SEVEN STORIES PRESS

NEW YORK • LONDON • MELBOURNE • TORONTO

A Seven Stories Press First Edition

Seven Stories Press
140 Watts Street
New York, NY 10013
www.sevenstories.com

In Canada: Publishers Group Canada, 559 College Street, Suite 402, Toronto, ON M6G 1A9

In the UK: Turnaround Publisher Services Ltd., Unit 3, Olympia Trading Estate, Coburg Road, Wood Green, London N22 6TZ

In Australia: Palgrave Macmillan, 15-19 Claremont Street, South Yarra, VIC 3141

College professors may order examination copies of Seven Stories Press titles for a free six-month trial period. To order, visit www.sevenstories.com/textbook or send a fax on school letterhead to (212) 226-1411.

Book design by Jon Gilbert

Library of Congress Cataloging-in-Publication Data

Sebald, Winfried Georg, 1944-2001.
    The emergence of memory : conversations with W.G. Sebald / edited by Lynne Sharon Schwartz. -- A Seven Stories Press 1st ed.
        p. cm
    ISBN 978-1-58322-785-5
1. Sebald, Winfried Georg, 1944-2001--Interviews. I. Schwartz, Lynne Sharon. II. Title.
    PT2681.E18Z46 2007
    833'.914--dc22
                                    2007025737
Printed in the USA.

9 8 7 6 5 4 3 2 1

Contents

Acknowledgments

I could not have completed this book without the extraordinary assistance of Arleen Zimmerle, reference librarian at Bryn Mawr College, whose proficiency, enthusiasm, esprit, and inexhaustible patience turned the search for materials on W. G. Sebald into an absorbing task. Not least among the discoveries I made over the course of our many Tuesday afternoons in the library was the pleasure of her company.

I was also assisted by the able and amiable Joe Tucker, reference librarian at Bennington College, who gave so promptly and generously of his time and knowledge. And by Elizabeth Catanes, a recent graduate of Bryn Mawr College, who was efficient, helpful, and undaunted by the labyrinths of the Internet.

Introduction

by Lynne Sharon Schwartz

W. G. Sebald's death in 2001 at the age of fifty-seven shocked his readers, certainly; it also left them feeling uncannily bereft. In the few years since *The Emigrants*, his first work translated from German into English, appeared in 1996, he had become, as if by stealth, an indispensable writer, one we could not afford to lose. More than anyone else writing today, he made it new. His undulating, hypnotic sentences (despite their antique cast) are paradigms of the modern sensibility, its tangled restlessness as well as its torpor. His dreamlike narratives, meandering yet meticulous, echo the lingering state of shock that is our legacy—not only from the wars of recent memory but from the century of colonialism that preceded them, indeed, history's "long account of calamities."

He made history new as well: the gaze that took in broad swathes of "the clearly chronic process of . . . impoverishment and degeneration" also resurrected them with heartbreaking lyrical precision. His language and breadth of vision combined in a slow burn, and by the light of that combustion we could glimpse what we have come from and what we have arrived at. Even, in a few dark, prophetic passages, where we're going: "For somehow we know by instinct that outsize buildings cast the shadow of their own destruction before them, and are designed from the first with an eye to their later existence as ruins." I found this in his last novel, *Austerlitz*, which I happened to open in mid-September of 2001—a coincidence eerily in keeping with Sebald's own broodings on serendipity across time and space, and on "the imponderables that govern our course through life."

The protagonist of *Austerlitz*, "entrusting" his life story to the narrator, begins with a curious remark: "Since my childhood and youth . . . I have never known who I really was." Sebald, though he had much in common with Jacques Austerlitz, in one sense knew exactly who he was, to his regret. In *Vertigo*, on hearing a bunch of rowdy German tourists beneath his Venetian hotel room, the narrator thinks, "How I wished during those sleepless hours that I belonged to a different nation, or, better still, to none at all."

He was born in 1944 in the small village of Wertagh im All-gäu in southern Bavaria, in the Alps near the Swiss border. He did not know his father, an officer in the Wehrmacht, until the latter returned from a prisoner-of-war camp in 1947. His closest attachment was to his maternal grandfather, a kindly man quite different from the austere, incurious father whom he could never forgive for his participation in the war and his later silence about it. His grandfather's death when Sebald was twelve was a blow from which he said he never recovered.

He studied German language and literature first at the University of Freiburg and then in Switzerland, but dissatisfaction, particularly with his ex-Nazi professors who never alluded to the immediate past, soon compelled him to leave the continent at twenty-one. He continued his studies in Manchester and remained in England; at the time of his death Sebald had been teaching for over thirty years at the University of East Anglia, where he was also the first director of the British Centre for Literary Translation. He was married and left a daughter who survived the auto accident that killed him.

Sebald wrote in his native German. In one of those enigmatic flukes of publishing, the order in which his books appeared in English is not the order in which they were written and published in German. In English, *The Emigrants* (1996), which won almost universal critical praise for its then unknown author, was followed by *The Rings of Saturn* in 1998, *Vertigo* in 1999, and *Austerlitz* in 2001. The long poem *After Nature*, which Sebald described as his first venture into nonacademic writing, appeared posthumously in 2002, and *On the Natural History of Destruction*, based on a 1997 series of lectures he gave in Zurich on the World War II destruction of German cities and the treatment of that subject—or, in his view, lack of treatment—by postwar German writers, in 2003. *Campo Santo* (2005), a collection of essays on his visits to Corsica as well as on various literary figures, was put together after his death.

In German, *After Nature* was published in 1988; it contains three sections, fictionalized riffs on the lives of Matthias Grünewald, the sixteenth-century German painter; Georg Wilhelm Steller, the eighteenth-century botanist; and Sebald himself. As for the prose works, if they are read in their order of composition, *Vertigo*, with its flights of invention taking off from the lives of Stendhal, Kafka, and Casanova, shows the tortuous, associative Sebald strategy on a relatively small scale, except for its extraordinary final section on the narrator's return visit to his native Bavaria, which gives a sense of postwar village life as it must have been during the author's childhood.

The Emigrants, which was written next, goes far more deeply into Sebald's primary theme of exile and displacement, with each of its four sections devoted to characters who were forced to leave Germany, three because they were Jewish and one for more subtle personal reasons. Three of the four stories end in suicide. Instead of so many losses becoming diminished in effect, each death adds weight to the grief of the next.

In *The Rings of Saturn,* to my mind Sebald's best work, his imagination is given free rein and his digressive bent carried to its most extreme—almost comic—reaches. The swirling paths of thought cast a spell: if the reader is willing to submit, the author's sensibility will carry him toward ever more tangled and distressing tales of decay, entropy, and destruction. The novel is shaped by a walking tour through the east of England; the narrator's initial search for the skull of Sir Thomas Browne (the seventeenth-century author of *Urn Burial*) leads circuitously to a meditation on Joseph Conrad, to Belgian atrocities in the Congo, to the execution of Roger Casement, to Swinburne and Edward FitzGerald, and eventually loops to silkworm cultivation in China and its spread through Europe during the Enlightenment.

The account of the Third Reich's promotion of the silk industry, like so much else in Sebald's work, becomes a metaphor for the unspeakable. Silkworm cultivation, according to the Nazis, will teach "the essential measures which are taken by breeders to monitor productivity and selection, including extermination to prevent racial degeneration." He goes on to describe how the cocoons are finally destroyed in rising steam: "When a batch is done, it is the next one's turn, and so on until the entire killing business is completed." As André Aciman pointed out in a 1998 essay, "Sebald never brings up the Holocaust. The reader, meanwhile, thinks of nothing else." (This was written before the publication of *Austerlitz*; there Sebald spends many pages on a detailed description of the camp at Terezin.)

Austerlitz is the closest Sebald comes to writing a "real" novel, with a protagonist driven to solve the mysteries of his lost past. Born in Prague, Jacques Austerlitz was evacuated by train at the age of four, along with other Jewish children, to escape the war. An emotionally frozen Welsh Calvinist couple raise him; in the silence and austerity of their airless house, he "forgets" his early years (much as the Germany of Sebald's youth managed to "forget" the recent past). When the "vortex of past time" becomes too turbulent, he suffers a breakdown: "I had neither memory nor the power of thought, nor even any existence . . . All my life had been a constant process of obliteration, a turning away from myself and the world."

Despite its having something resembling a plot, *Austerlitz* is typically meditative, digressive, undramatic, and shuns the techniques of the realistic novel, a genre for which Sebald felt impatience, even some contempt, as will be seen in the interviews. *Austerlitz* is my favorite after *The Rings of Saturn*, perhaps because as a novelist myself, I enjoy seeing how Sebald remakes the genre on his own terms. Some critics, though, including Arthur Lubow in the interview that follows, sense in *Austerlitz* "the author's unconventional mind creaking against the walls of convention." And Michael Hofmann finds the story "inevitably trite."

Like many writers of genius, Sebald dwells always on the same large themes. His favorite is the swift blossoming of every human endeavor and its long slow death, either through natural or man-made disaster, leaving a wealth of remains to be pored over, not to mention vast human suffering. His notions of time make this panoramic view possible. Like the spectral wanderers of his novels—all of them facets of Sebald himself, the prism—he sees time as plastic, irregular, subjective, "a disquiet of the mind." Only our panic willfully orders it by the movements of the planets. Past and present might be concurrent or not, might stop and start with the erratic spasms of the mind, of memory. Why might we not have "appointments to keep in the past" just as we do in the future? But in our collective amnesia, we erase time as we go, forgetting what defines us. He has not forgotten; he pieces together the shards to remind us. And by some unfathomable sleight of hand, in making things clear and whole, he gives them the luster of mystery.

The Sebald narrator is a wanderer, by train through Italian cities and New York suburbs, on foot through the empty reaches of the English countryside, exploring the history of each settlement he passes through. He spends sleepless, despairing nights in bleak hotel rooms, frequently in a state of emotional or physical collapse. Wherever he travels, he finds strangely vacant streets and roads, not a soul around. He sees apparitions, figures from history gliding by. He visits deserted museums, "collections of oddities"; he photographs landscapes, streets, monuments, ticket stubs. Sebald's books are famously strewn with evocative, gloomy black-and-white photographs that call up the presence of the dead, of vanished places, and also serve as proofs of his passage.

Like the author, the narrator is German and left home young. Returning to his native town revives the unease—even disgust—that made him leave: "I felt increasingly that the mental impoverishment and lack of memory that marked the Germans, and the efficiency with which they had cleaned everything up, were beginning to affect my head and my nerves." Sometimes he visits or merely recalls an old friend, and we hear the friend's story, very like his own, in a voice like his own. All Sebald's characters sound like the narrator; as he explains in Arthur Lubow's interview, "it's all relayed through this narrative figure. It's as he remembers, so it's in his cast."

Among the relentless examples of "the insatiable urge for destruction," the most urgent is the physical and metaphysical damage of the war waged by the Reich. With his enveloping suspicion of something having been hidden from him and the resulting sense of alienation, a theme he returns to frequently in the interviews, it is hardly surprising that Sebald became the chronicler of the displaced, the exiles, those who imagine, like Jacques Austerlitz, that they are living the wrong life, who sense a ghostly twin beside them.

Sebald was exceptionally fortunate in his English translators, Michael Hulse and Anthea Bell, with whom he collaborated closely and whose task cannot have been simple, given the length and elaborate—one might say baroque, even perverse—architecture of his sentences. Michael Hulse translated *The Emigrants*, *The Rings of Saturn*, and *Vertigo*. Anthea Bell translated *Austerlitz*, *On the Natural History of Destruction*, and *Campo Santo*. The poet Michael Hamburger, who was a friend of Sebald's and also appears as a character in *The Rings of Saturn*, translated the poems *After Nature* and *Unrecounted* (also published posthumously). All three make the books read as if they were conceived and written in English; there can be no higher achievement for a translator.

Because Sebald invented a new form of prose writing that makes tangible the contemporary blurring of borders between fiction and nonfiction, critics have puzzled over what to call his

works, with their mélange of fictionalized memoir, travel journals, inventories of natural and man-made curiosities,
impressionistic musings on painting, entomology, architecture,
military fortifications, and more. Sebald himself used the term
prose narratives. Baffling classification, they take the shape of
the author's consciousness. What unifies them is the narrator's
distilled voice—melancholy, resonant as a voice in a tunnel,
witty: the effluvia of their author's inner life. And against all
odds, from these stories of exile and decay, the voice wrests a
magical exhilaration. Several of the writers included here mention the urge to go back and read his books over as soon as they
reach the final page. They are not only magnetic, drawing you
back. They are evanescent, evaporating as the pages turn,
exactly like the lives and settings they brood on. As Sebald
writes of a landscape "dissolved in a pearl-gray haze": "it was
the very evanescence of these visions that gave me, at the time,
something like a sense of eternity."

Always, the world is veiled, seen through fog and mist: a "veil
of rain," a "veil of ash," "a profusion of dusty glitter." An exiled
German painter in *The Emigrants* loves the accumulation of
dust in his studio, "the grey, velvety sinter left when matter dissolved, little by little into nothingness." After a dust storm, the
narrator observes, "although it now grew lighter once more, the
sun, which was at its zenith, remained hidden behind the banners of pollen-fine dust that hung for a long time in the air.
This, I thought, will be what is left after the earth had ground
itself down." Instead of feeling crushed by the image, we feel
oddly sustained. It is the sustenance offered by truth, however
somber.

In several of the interviews that follow, Sebald mentions the
porousness of the border between the worlds of the living and

the dead; in parts of Corsica, he says, people imagine the dead returning to get a piece of bread from the pantry. As a boy, Jacques Austerlitz listens to the village cobbler's tales of seeing the dead "who had been struck down by fate untimely . . . marching up the hill above the town to the soft beat of a drum." The cobbler shows the boy a piece of black veil his grandfather saved from one of their biers: "Nothing but a piece of silk like that separates us from the next world."

Sebald makes Austerlitz's story passionately lucid. What is perplexing is the narrator's relationship to him. Gradually that, too, comes to light. Austerlitz "must find someone to whom he could tell his own story . . . and for which he needed the kind of listener I had been." In the interviews, Sebald speaks of the ambiguous position of the listener absorbing the exiles' stories until he takes on the burden of the tale. More than mere witness, by his unstinting attention he shares, if not the storyteller's fate, at least his memory. Toward the end of his story, Austerlitz gives the narrator the key to his apartment, passing on his life for safekeeping. The novel is the key Sebald passes on to us.

In an essay on the work of Peter Weiss, Sebald writes that "the artistic self engages personally in . . . a reconstruction, pledging itself . . . to set up a memorial, and the painful nature of that process could be said to ensure the continuance of memory." He repeats this more poignantly in *The Emigrants*, in the voice of the exiled Max Ferber, who leaves the narrator a memento, along with words that augur the task Sebald assumed in his writing. His mother's memoirs, Ferber says, "had seemed to him like one of those evil German fairy tales in which, once you are under the spell, you have to carry on to the finish, till your heart breaks, with whatever work you have begun—in this case, the remembering, writing and reading. That is why I would rather you took this package."

I chose the pieces that follow from an enormous number of interviews, reviews, and essays; many major American and British critics and novelists have been moved to write about Sebald—and no wonder, given his originality and his sudden appearance, fully formed, as if out of nowhere. As a rule I don't cherish interviews: I find writers explaining themselves and their methods not only less interesting and polished than the works themselves, but also less trustworthy. In the case of Sebald, however, like many other readers, I felt cheated out of those unborn books that surely would have given more of what Stephen Daedalus called "enchantment of the heart." I had expected to be reading new ones for years to come.

The interviews do indeed offer more: his preoccupations, his literary forebears and tastes, his background, and the sources of his grave outlook, that insistence on probing "the traces of decay." They have the added curiosity of showing how Sebald sounds extemporaneously—quite different from the elaborately webbed constructs in his writing. He is more colloquial than one might expect; he is also incisive and direct, cooperative and adaptable. That is, in almost Zelig-like fashion, he adapts his responses to the tone of the interviewer. Where I anticipated a grim reserve, even taciturnity or grumpiness, he is congenial. Listening to him on tape reveals a low, gravelly voice, serious, occasionally ponderous, but more often witty and at times even verging on the lighthearted.

In interviews of this kind there is bound to be some repetition, and at first I planned to edit this out. Thinking it over, though, I decided that the recurrence of certain themes was useful: it demonstrates to what extent Sebald was possessed, even haunted, by specific motifs from his life and the life of his country. For Germany, which he left so early on, is his country, as he says in Eleanor Wachtel's interview, whether he likes it or not, and he does not like it. Sooner or later, in most of the interviews, will arise his abhorrence of his parents' silence about the war and, by extension, of his country's "collective amnesia." Inevitably, too, he talks about his frustrating university days, where he sensed something amiss in his professors' evasion of the past (elsewhere, less discreetly, he calls them "dissembling old Nazis"); about the difficulty of writing, especially the moral ambiguities involved in the kind of writing he did; about the destruction of the natural world and the graceless incursions of technology; about the overriding significance of memory.

Eleanor Wachtel's and Carole Angier's interviews took place in 1997, when only *The Emigrants* had been published, in English. Angier's appeared in *The Jewish Quarterly* and concentrates on the Jewish characters in that book—all based on people Sebald knew—and on his relation to them and their stories. Wachtel's is concerned with the form and sources of the book and examines the background of its real-life models. Arthur Lubow visited Sebald in Norwich in August 2001 in preparation for an essay whose publication was delayed because of the September 11 attacks and finally came out in truncated form three days before Sebald's death. What appears here is Lubow's fuller description of their encounter, reinterpreted with unfortunate hindsight. Joseph Cuomo's wide-ranging conversation with Sebald in March 2001 was preceded by the author's reading from *The Rings of Saturn* as part of the Queens College Evening Readings series. From that late vantage point, it covers almost all of his work, its major themes and ramifications. Michael Silverblatt's radio interview was done in November 2001, a month before Sebald's death; it focuses on his style and its derivations, and has crucial insights into Sebald's relation to his subject, particularly the victims of Nazi atrocities.

I chose the four essays with a view to offering cogent accounts of almost all of Sebald's books. Ruth Franklin's deals in detail with *After Nature* and *On the Natural History of Destruction*; Charles Simic's discusses the latter book, among others; and Tim Parks's concentrates on *Vertigo*. All three view his themes in the broadest possible of contexts and also shed light on the ambiguities and perils implicit in his approach and his subject matter. Franklin's piece, in particular, points out the risks involved in what she sees as Sebald's aestheticizing of collective disaster and outlines, with admirable evenhandedness, her discomfort with his handling of the air war against Germany.

On the Natural History of Destruction aroused controversy when it was published on the grounds that Sebald did not place his account of German suffering in the larger context of Germany's aggression. I believe that Sebald assumed—maybe too naively—that his readers would supply the context, and in fact he says as much in the postscript he added later. The remoteness or coldness critics have noted evinces savage indignation under tight control, especially in his critiques of postwar German writers; the words seem to emerge through gritted teeth. I suspect Sebald is expressing his own view in *Austerlitz*, when we hear, thirdhand, that the protagonist's father, killed by the Nazis, "did not in any way believe that the German people had been driven into their misfortune; rather, in his view, they had entirely re-created themselves in this perverse form, engendered by every individual's wishful thinking . . . and had then brought forth, as symbolic exponents of their innermost desires, so to speak, the Nazi grandees."

Charles Simic's piece takes the opposite view of Franklin's, and I felt it useful to set these two persuasive arguments side by side. Simic also places the destruction of the German cities in a historical context—the ceaseless killing of civilians in warfare, up to the present venture in Iraq.

Finally, I was drawn to these writers because they connect Sebald's themes to events in their own lives—Simic to his childhood experience of war, Franklin to the loss of family members, and Parks to a piquant personal memory that echoes Sebald's fascination with coincidence. Parks, incidentally, is the only writer to mention Sebald's humor, which glimmers slyly through his pessimism and is often overlooked. (Joseph Cuomo's interview is punctuated by bursts of laughter from the audience at Sebald's wry remarks and deadpan delivery.)

Michael Hofmann's provocative essay—the one dissenting voice—is included as a skeptical corrective to what might otherwise be a gush of nearly unqualified enthusiasm. The vulnerabilities in Sebald that he spears so pointedly, as well as the gothic elements, are real and should be taken into account in any assessment of his work.

To help make such an assessment, and to keep us remembering him, it seemed fitting to let Sebald have this final word—or rather, these many final words. He was, after all, an essential guardian of historical memory, dedicated to seeing that the ravages and casualties of history do not evaporate like the fog he was so fond of. This he did, not with any optimistic notion of progress or reform, but for the integrity of the act itself, and for the satisfaction of resurrecting what has been lost in language that would endure.

The Hunter

by Tim Parks

In the closing pages of Cervantes's masterpiece, at last disabused and disillusioned, a decrepit Don Quixote finds that there is nothing for him beyond folly but death. When giants are only windmills and Dulcinea a stout peasant lass who has no time for a knight errant, life, alas, is unlivable. "Truly he is dying," says the priest who takes his confession, "and truly he is sane." Sancho Panza breaks down in tears: "Oh don't die, dear master! . . . Take my advice and live many years. For the maddest thing a man can do in this life is to let himself die just like that, without anybody killing him, but just finished off by his own melancholy."

Centuries later, observing the loss of all illusion that he felt characterized the modern world, the melancholic Giacomo Leopardi wrote: "Everything is folly but folly itself." And again a hundred and more years later, the arch pessimist Emil Cioran rephrased the reflection thus: "The true vertigo is the absence of folly." What makes Don Quixote so much luckier than Leopardi and Cioran, and doubtless Cervantes himself, is that, as the epitaph on his tombstone puts it, "he had the luck . . . to live a fool and yet die wise." What on earth would have become of such a sentimental idealist had he returned to his senses, as it were, a decade or two earlier?

Originally appeared in *The New York Review of Books*, June 15, 2000. Reprinted with permission from *The New York Review of Books*. © 2000 NYREV, Inc.

Both in *Vertigo* and in his later novels *The Emigrants* and *The Rings of Saturn*, W. G. Sebald tells the stories of those who reach disillusionment long before the flesh is ready to succumb. The men in his book—they are always men—are engaged in a virtuoso struggle to conjure within themselves the minimum of folly, or we could call it love of life or even engagement, that will prevent them from dying "just like that," "finished off by [their] own melancholy."

But perhaps I have got that wrong. For it could also be said that Sebald's characters are men who ruthlessly suppress folly the moment it raises its irrepressible head. So wary are they of engagement in life that they are morbidly and masochistically in complicity with melancholy and all too ready to be over-whelmed by it. There is a back and forth in Sebald's work between the wildest whimsy and the bleakest realism. One extreme calls to the other: the illusions of passion, in the past; a quiet suicide, all too often, in the future. Mediating between the two, images both of his art and of what fragile nostalgic equilibrium may be available to his heroes, are the grainy black-and-white photographs Sebald scatters throughout his books. Undeniably images of *something*, something real that is, they give documentary evidence of experiences that, as we will discover in the text, sparked off in the narrator or hero a moment of mental excitement, of mystery, or folly, or alarm. They are the wherewithal of an enchantment, at once feared and desired, and above all necessary for staying alive. Not even in the grainiest of these photos, however, will it be possible to mistake a windmill for a giant.

There are four pieces in *Vertigo*. All of them involve a back and forth across the Alps between northern Europe and Italy. The first is entitled "Beyle, or Love is a Madness Most Discreet,"

and it is the only one to offer something like the whole trajectory of a life through passion and engagement to disillusionment
and depression. By using Stendhal's baptismal name, Marie-
Henri Beyle, Sebald alerts us at once, and far more effectively
than if he had used the writer's pseudonym, to the extent to
which identity is invented as well as given and thus involves con-
tinuous effort. Beyle created Stendhal, as Señor Quesada
dreamed up Don Quixote. Taking on the identity was one with
the folly, its most positive achievement perhaps. But that is not to
say that Beyle, whoever he was, did not live on, as even Quesada
reemerged for extreme unction.

In his opening sentence Sebald likes to give us a strong cocktail of date, place, and purposeful action. Thus the Beyle piece
begins: "In mid-May of the year 1800 Napoleon and a force of
36,000 men crossed the Great St. Bernard pass. . . ." The second
piece starts: "In October 1980 I travelled from England . . . to
Vienna, hoping that a change of place would help me get over a
particularly difficult period in my life." And the third: "On Sat-
urday the 6th of September, 1913, Dr. K., the Deputy Secretary
of the Prague Workers' Insurance Company, is on his way to
Vienna to attend a congress on rescue services and hygiene."

It is so concrete, so promising! All too soon, however, and
this is one of the most effective elements of comedy in Sebald's
work, the concrete will become elusive; the narrative momentum is dispersed in a delta as impenetrable as it is fertile. Thus
Beyle, who at age seventeen was with Napoleon on that "mem-
orable" crossing, finds it impossible, at age fifty-three, to arrive
at a satisfactory recollection of events. "At times his view of the
past consists of nothing but grey patches, then at others images
appear of such extraordinary clarity he feels he can scarce
credit them." He is right not to. His vivid memory of General

Marmont beside the mountain track wearing the sky-blue robes of a councillor must surely be wrong, since Marmont was a general at the time and would thus have been wearing his general's uniform. If crossing the St. Bernard with an army was, as Sebald concludes his opening sentence, "an undertaking that had been regarded until that time as next to impossible," remembering that undertaking, even for a man with a mind as formidable as Stendhal's, turns out to be not only "next to" but truly impossible.

This is hardly news. That the difficulty of every act of memory has a way of drawing our attention to the perversity of the mind and the complicity between its creative and corrosive powers is a commonplace. "*And the last remnants memory destroys,*" we read beneath the title of one of the pieces in *The Emigrants*. No, it is Sebald's sense of the role of this act of fickle memory in the overall trajectory of his characters' lives that makes the pieces in *Vertigo* so engaging and convincing.

Beyle/Stendhal's life as described by Sebald is as follows. Crossing the Alps, the adolescent dragoon is appalled by the dead horses along the wayside but later cannot remember why: "His impressions had been erased by the very violence of their impact." Arriving in Italy he sees a performance of Cimarosa's *Il matrimonio segreto*, falls wildly in love with a plain if not ugly prima donna, overspends on fashionable clothes, and finally "disburdens" himself of his virginity with a prostitute. "Afterwards," we are told, "he could no longer recall the name or face of the *donna cattiva* who had assisted him in this task." The word "task" appears frequently and comically in *Vertigo*, most often in Thomas Bernhard's sense of an action that one is simply and irrationally compelled to do, not a social duty or act of gainful employment.

Despite contracting syphilis in the city's brothels, Beyle cultivates "a passion of a more abstract nature" for the mistress of a fellow soldier. She ignores him, but eleven years later, deploying an "insane loquacity," he convinces her to yield on the condition that he will then leave Milan at once. Exhilarated by his conquest, Beyle is overcome by melancholy. He sees *Il matrimonio segreto* again and is entirely unimpressed by a most beautiful prima donna. Visiting the battlefield at Marengo, the discrepancy between his frequent imaginings of the heroic battle and the actual presence of the bleached bones of thousands of corpses produces a frightening vertigo, after which the shabby monument to the fallen can only make a mean impression. Again he embarks on a romantic passion, this time for the wife of a Polish officer. His mad indiscretion leads her to reject him, but he retains a plaster cast of her hand (we see a photograph) that was to mean "as much to him as Métilde herself could ever have done."

Sebald now concentrates on Beyle's account of his romantic attachment to one Madame Gherardi, a "mysterious, not to say unearthly figure," who may in fact have been only (only!) a figment of his imagination. Usually skeptical of his romantic vision of love, one day this "phantom" lady does at last speak "of a divine happiness beyond comparison with anything else in life." Overcome by "dread" Beyle backs off. The long last paragraph of the piece begins: "Beyle wrote his great novels between 1829 and 1842, plagued constantly by the symptoms of syphilis."

The trajectory is clear enough. The effort of memory and of writing begins, it seems, where the intensities of romance and military glory end. It is the "task" of the disillusioned, at once a consolation and a penance. In 1829 Beyle turned forty-seven.

Sebald turned forty-seven in 1990, the year in which *Vertigo*, his first "novel," was published. Coincidences are important in this writer's work. Why?

The Beyle piece is followed by an account of two journeys Sebald himself made in 1980 and 1987 to Venice, Verona, and Lake Garda (all places visited by Stendhal). The third piece describes a similar journey apparently made by Kafka in the fall of 1913, exactly a hundred years after the French writer reports having visited the lake with the mysterious Madame Gherardi. As Stendhal was referred to only by his baptismal name and not the name he invented, so Kafka, in what is the most fantastical and "poetic" piece in the book, is referred to only as K., the name used for the protagonists of *The Trial* and *The Castle*. Or not quite. In fact, Sebald refers to him as "Dr. K., Deputy Secretary of the Prague Workers' Insurance Company," thus bringing together Kafka's "professional" existence as an insurance broker and his fictitious creation, begging the question of the "identity" of the man who lies between the two.

Beginning in Verona, the last piece, "Il ritorno in patria," shows the author interrupting "my various tasks" to undertake a journey that will take him back to the village of his childhood in Alpine Bavaria, where most of the piece is set, and finally on to England, where Sebald has his "professional" existence as a university lecturer. In all three of these pieces the romantic and military adventures of the young Henri Beyle are very much behind our now decidedly melancholic characters, and yet they are ever present too. As if between Scylla and Charybdis, when Dr. K. sits down to eat at the sanitarium on Lake Garda, it is to find an aging general on one side and an attractive young lady on the other.

Similarly, on returning to the building where he grew up, Sebald remembers his boyhood longing for the company of the pretty waitress in the bar on the ground floor and the fact that he was forbidden to visit the top floor because of the mysterious presence of a "grey *chasseur*," presumably a ghost, in the attic. Satisfying his curiosity forty years later, the narrator climbs to the attic to discover a tailor's dummy dressed in the military uniform of the Austrian *chasseurs*. It is hard to steer a course across the wild waters generated by these two somehow complicitous follies. Was it not after all a combination of distressed damsels and military grandeur that overwhelmed Don Quixote's sanity? *Vertigo* offers a number of images of ships heading for shipwrecks.

But the question of coincidences keeps turning up. In the second piece, entitled "All'estero" ("Abroad"), we are introduced to a character who could not be further from Sebald's usually melancholic type, Giovanni Casanova. So far we have heard how the writer, in deep depression, travels from England to Vienna, falls into a state of mental paralysis, and is on the brink of becoming down-and-out when in desperation he sets out for Venice, a city so labyrinthine that "you cannot tell what you will see next or indeed who will see you the very next moment." One of the things he sees of course in Venice is the Doge's Palace, which causes him to think of Casanova.

With admirable reticence, Sebald has given us no reason for the cause of his depression. But if only because we have just read the Beyle piece, and there are various tiny hints scattered here and there, we suspect that romance is at least part of the problem, or, as Dr. K. will think of it in the following piece: the impossibility of leading "the only possible life, to live together with a woman, each one free and independent." Just to see the name Casanova, then, to think of that great seducer and endlessly resourceful schemer, produces a fierce contrast. Yet even Casanova experienced a period of depression and mental paralysis. When? When, like some hero of Kafka's, he was imprisoned without explanation in the Doge's Palace. And how did he escape? With the help of a coincidence.

In order to decide on what day he would attempt to break out of his cell, Casanova used a complicated random system to consult *Orlando Furioso*, thus, incredibly, happening on the words: "Between the end of October and the beginning of November." The escape was successful. Casanova fled to France, where he later invented for himself the identity Chevalier de Seingalt. But just as remarkable as this propitious consultation of *Orlando Furioso* is the fact that October 31 turns out to be the very day upon which our author finds himself in Venice. Sebald is amazed, alarmed, fascinated.

Again and again it is coincidence, or uncanny repetition, those most evident outcroppings of the underlying mysteriousness of existence, that jerks the melancholic out of his paralysis. It is as if, disillusioned to the point where certain follies have become unthinkable (and contemporary Europe, as Sebald showed in *The Emigrants*, has good reason for being thus disillusioned), we can only be set in motion by a fascination with life's mysteries, which are simply forced upon us in all sorts of ways. Between, or perhaps after, passion and glory lie the uncertain resource of curiosity, the recurring emotions of amazement and alarm. Any act of remembering will offer a feast.

Toward that midnight between October and November, Sebald rows out on the Venetian lagoon with an acquaintance who points out the city incinerator, the fires of which burn in perpetuity, and explains that he has been thinking a great deal about death and resurrection. "He had no answers," Sebald writes, "but believed the questions were quite sufficient to him." It is an echo, conscious or otherwise, of Rilke's advice to his "young poet" to "have patience with everything unresolved and try to love the questions themselves." Rilke was another German writer who had considerable problems both with military academies and with love.

But it would be a mistake to imagine that Sebald presents coincidence in a positive light. Extraordinary parallels may, briefly, release the paralyzed mind from its cell, get it sorting through old diaries, or tracking down books in libraries, or comically attempting on a bus, as in Sebald's case, to take photographs of twin boys who exactly resemble the adolescent Kafka, but they do this in the way that an alarm or a siren might. There is a destructive side to coincidence. It has a smell of death about it. What is the night "between the end of October and the beginning of November," if not the night before All Saints' Day, *I morti*, the Day of the Dead?

Why is this? To "coincide" is "to occupy the same place or time," says Chambers's dictionary, "to correspond, to be identical." The coincidence that Stendhal, Kafka, and Sebald all take similar trips at similar times of year, the first two exactly a century apart, may set curiosity in motion, but it also removes uniqueness from these events; the recurrence diminishes the original, replaces it, falsifies it, the way Beyle reports finding his memories of landscapes destroyed by their painterly representations, the way even an old photograph may be considered as stealing something of its original.

Here we are approaching the core of Sebald's vision, the spring at once of his pessimism, comedy, and lyricism. Engagement in the present inevitably involves devouring the past.

Waking up in his Venice hotel on November 1, remarking on the silence, Sebald contrasts it to the ceaseless surging of traffic he hears in the hotels of other cities, the endless oceanic roar of cars and trucks released wave upon wave from traffic lights. He concludes his description: "For some time now I have been convinced that it is out of this din that the life is being born which will come after us and will spell our gradual destruction, just as we have been gradually destroying what was there long before us." To be set, with Casanova, in motion, is to be returned to the business of destruction. The *chasseur*, or hunter, he who consumes his own sport (and what was Casanova if not a hunter?), is a recurring figure in this book. Occasionally Sebald hears his arrow whistle past an ear.

It is uncanny, on reading a work that makes so much of coincidences, to find it coinciding in an unsettling way with one's own life. Enviably adept at finding images and anecdotes that will deliver his vision, Sebald now tells us of his experiences in Verona, the town where I have lived for almost twenty years. Eating in a gloomy pizzeria, he is unsettled by the painting of a ship in peril on stormy seas. Trying to distract himself he reads an article in the paper about the so-called *caso* Ludwig. For some years a string of local murders were accompanied by the claims of a group calling itself Ludwig. Some of the victims were prostitutes, and there were incendiary attacks on discotheques which the murderers felt to be dens of sin. Again the sexual and the military seemed to have combined in the most disturbing fashion. How could Sebald not be appalled by the macabre German connection? And when the waiter brings his bill, he reads in the small print (again we have a reproduction) that the restaurant owner is one "Carlo Cadavero." This is too much, and the author flees on the night train to Innsbruck.

Aside from the fact that I was able to look up Carlo Cadavero's name in the Verona phone book, what struck me as uncanny was a comment from later in this piece where, returning to Verona seven years later, Sebald hears how the two adolescents, Wolfgang Abel and Marco Furlan, who created this terrible identity Ludwig, a sort of negative two-man Don Quixote, were tried and imprisoned. He remarks that although the evidence against them was "irrefutable," "the investigation produced nothing that might have made it possible to comprehend a series of crimes extending over almost seven years."

Irrefutable? It would have been about the same time as Sebald's second trip that, while carrying out English oral exams at the University of Verona, I found myself looking at the ID of a young woman whose surname was Furlan. Seeing my eyebrows rise, she said, "Yes, I am his sister. And he is innocent." She then went on to pass her exam, a conversation test, in exemplary fashion explaining to me with the utmost conviction that the whole thing was absurd and her brother the sweetest, most normal person on earth. Despite the irrefutable evidence, she believed this, as no doubt the sisters of those who later commit war crimes believe in all honesty that they are growing up in the most normal of families. They are. Not for nothing is Sebald's writing frequently set alight with images of terrible conflagrations that inexplicably consume everything, leaving the world to start again from under a veil of ash. Never mentioned, Shiva presides.

The time has come to say something about this writer's extraordinary prose, without which his rambling plots and

ruminations would be merely clever and unsettling. Like the
coincidences he speaks of, it is a style that recovers, devours,
and displaces the past. He has Thomas Bernhard's love of the
alarming superlative, the tendency to describe states of the
most devastating confusion with great precision and control.
But the touch is much lighter than Bernhard's, the instrument
more flexible. Kafka is present here too, perhaps from time to
time Robert Walser, and no doubt others as well. But all these
predecessors have been completely digested, destroyed, and
remade in Sebald and above all in his magnificent descriptions,
which mediate so effectively between casual incident and grand
reflection. One suspects too that Michael Hulse's translation,
which possesses a rare internal coherence of register and
rhythm, is itself the product of a long process of digestion and
recasting, a wonderful, as it were, coincidence. Some of the
English is breathtaking. All the same, the most effective
moments are often the more modest stylistically. Here is the
author in a railway carriage with two beautiful women; knowing what we know of him, any approach to them is impossible,
yet how attractive they are in their mystery!

> Outside, in the slanting sunlight of late afternoon, the
> poplars and fields of Lombardy went by. Opposite me
> sat a Franciscan nun of about thirty or thirty-five and a
> young girl with a colorful patchwork jacket over her
> shoulders. The girl had got on at Brescia, while the nun
> had already been on the train at Desenzano. The nun
> was reading her breviary, and the girl, no less immersed,
> was reading a photo story. Both were consummately
> beautiful, both very much present and yet altogether
> elsewhere. I admired the profound seriousness with

which each of them turned the pages. Now the Franciscan nun would turn a page over, now the girl in the colorful jacket, then the girl again and then the Franciscan nun once more. Thus the time passed without my ever being able to exchange a glance with either the one or the other. I therefore tried to practice a like modesty, and took out *Der Beredte Italiener*, a handbook published in 1878 in Berne, for all who wish to make speedy and assured progress in colloquial Italian.

Only Sebald, one suspects, would study an out-of-date phrase book while missing the chance to speak to two attractive ladies. The determinedly old-fashioned aura that hangs about all his prose is part and parcel of his decidedly modern version of non-engagement. Yet from the "insane loquacity" of the romantic Beyle to the charming picture in the book's last piece of Sebald enamored of his teacher and "filling my exercise books with a web of lines and numbers in which I hoped to entangle Fraulein Rauch forever," few writers make us more aware of the seductive powers of language. Sebald's literary enticements seek to achieve an intimacy that will not be so destructive as other follies: the direct encounter, the hunter's knife. This truly is a "madness most discreet."

All of which leads us to the only possible objection that I can imagine being raised against this remarkable writer. That to succumb to his seduction is to resign oneself to more of the same: the broken lives, the coincidences, these unhappy men and enigmatic women. Is it a problem? With his accustomed blend of slyness and grim comedy, Sebald tackles the issue himself in a section from the last piece of *Vertigo*. Sitting in the hotel in the Bavarian village of his childhood, he observes a

gloomy painting depicting woodcutters at work and recalls that
the artist, Hengge, was famous for his pictures of woodcutters.
"His murals, always in dark shades of brown, were to be seen
on the walls of buildings all around W. and the surrounding
area, and were always of his favored motifs." The author sets
out to tramp around the surrounding woods and villages to
rediscover all these paintings, finding them "most unsettling,"
which is to say, for Sebald, good, since only what is unsettling
attracts his attention, heightens sensibility, warns of life's dan-
gers, recuperates its horrors in pathos. He then gives us the
following comment on Hengge's tendency always to paint the
same subject, ending with a moment of alarming but also
amusing vertigo, that dizzying empty space that Sebald finds
at the core of every intensity:

> Hengge the painter was perfectly capable of extending
> his repertoire. But whenever he was able to follow his
> own artistic inclination, he would paint only pictures
> of woodcutters. Even after the war, when for a variety
> of reasons his monumental works were no longer
> much in demand, he continued in the same vein. In the
> end, his house was said to have been so crammed with
> pictures of woodcutters that there was scarcely room
> for Hengge himself, and death, so the obituary said,
> caught him in the midst of a work showing a woodcut-
> ter on a sledge hurtling down into the valley below.

As long as Sebald shows this kind of resourcefulness, my
only regret, when his task obliges him to repeat himself, will be
the tendency of the new book to eclipse the old.

Ghost Hunter

by Eleanor Wachtel

ELEANOR WACHTEL: Sebald writes a requiem for a generation in *The Emigrants*, an extraordinary book about memory, exile, and death. The writing is lyrical, the mood elegiac. These are stories of absence and displacement, loss and suicide, Germans and Jews, written in the most evocative, haunting, and understated way. *The Emigrants* is variously called a novel, a narrative quartet, or simply unclassifiable. How would you describe it?

W. G. SEBALD: It's a form of prose fiction. I imagine it exists more frequently on the European continent than in the Anglo-Saxon world, i.e., dialogue plays hardly any part in it at all. Everything is related round various corners in a periscopic sort of way. In that sense it doesn't conform to the patterns that standard fiction has established. There isn't an authorial narrator. And there are various limitations of this kind that seem to push the book into a special category. But what exactly to call it, I don't know.

EW: You've put together four stories of four different lives that have connections and resonate but seem to be discrete in the telling. Why did you want to write about them together in *The Emigrants*?

A version of this interview, recorded on October 16, 1997, was broadcast on CBC Radio's *Writers & Company* on April 18, 1998, and produced by Sandra Rabinovitch.

WGS: Because the patterns are remarkably similar. They are all stories about suicide or, to be more precise, suicides at an advanced age, which is relatively rare but quite frequent as a symptom of what we know as the survivor syndrome.

I was familiar with that particular symptom in the abstract, through such cases as Jean Améry, Primo Levi, Paul Celan, Tadeusz Borowski, and various others who failed to escape the shadows which were cast over their lives by the Shoah and ultimately succumbed to the weight of memory. That tends to happen quite late in these people's lives, when they're in retirement age, as it were, when all of a sudden some kind of void opens up. The duties of professional life recede into the background and then, you know, time for thought is there all of a sudden. As I was working at one point round about 1989, 1990 on Jean Améry in particular because he originated from an area not far from the area in which I grew up, it occurred to me that in fact I did know four people who fitted that particular category almost exactly. And it was at that point that I became preoccupied with these lives, started looking into them, traveled, tried to find all the traces I could possibly find, and in the end, had to write this down.

The stories as they appear in the book follow pretty much the lines or the trajectories of these four lives as they were in reality. The changes that I made, i.e., extending certain vectors, foreshortening certain things, adding here and there, taking something away, are marginal changes, changes of style rather than changes of substance. In the first three stories there is almost a one-to-one relationship between these lives and the lives of the people I knew. In the case of the fourth story I used two different foils, one of a painter who currently still works in England and the other a landlord I had in Manchester when I first moved there. And because the landlord I had in Manchester is still alive today, I didn't want him to appear, as it were, in an undisguised form in what is essentially a work of documentary fiction, so I introduced this second foil in order to make it less obvious. But they're pretty much the same life stations that these people went through that I knew very well.

EW: You say at one point that it's "as if the dead were coming back, or as if we were on the point of joining them." This idea seems to preoccupy you.

WGS: Well, I don't quite know what the reason for that is, except that death entered my own life at a very early point. I grew up in a very small village, very high up in the Alps, about three thousand feet above sea level. And in the immediate post-war years when I grew up there, it was in many ways quite an archaic place. For instance, you couldn't bury the dead in the winter because the ground was frozen and there was no way of digging it up. So you had to leave them in the woodshed for a month or two until the thaw came. You grew up with this knowledge that death is around you, and when and if someone died, it happened in the middle or in the center of the house, as it were, the dead person went through their agonies in the living room, and then before the burial they would be still part of the family for possibly three, four days. So I was from a very early point on very familiar, much more familiar than people are nowadays, with the dead and the dying. I have always had at the back of my mind this notion that of course these people aren't really gone, they just hover somewhere at the perimeter of our lives and keep coming in on brief visits. And photographs are for me, as it were, one of the emanations of the dead, especially these older photographs of people no longer with us. Nevertheless, through these pictures, they do have what seems to me some sort of a spectral presence. And I've always been intrigued by that. It's got nothing to do with the mystical or the mysterious. It is just a remnant of a much more archaic way of looking at things.

If you go for instance to a place like Corsica . . . Nowadays of course it's not quite the same any more, but very recently, twenty years ago, the dead in Corsican culture had an unquestioned presence in the lives of the living. They were always reckoned with, they were always seen to be just round the corner, they were always seen to be coming into the house of an evening to get a crust of bread or to march down the main street as a gang with drums and fifes. And in more atavistic cultures, of which there were pockets in Europe until, I would think, about the 1960s, there is always a presence of these departed. And certainly there were areas in the Alps in the postwar years where that was also the case. Now it's all obliterated, of course. But somehow it got stuck in my mind, and I think it's possibly from that quarter that my preoccupation stems.

EW: You include many photographs with your text—of the people, the places, cityscapes or landscapes, and they're very evocative, they're haunting. In the narrative they seem to trigger a search. You see a photograph or you look at an album or someone shows you something, and then that takes you somewhere.

WGS: Well, the pictures have a number of different sources of origin and also a number of different purposes. But the majority of the photographs do come from the albums that certainly middle-class people kept in the thirties and forties. And they are from the authentic source. Ninety percent of the images inserted into the text could be said to be authentic, i.e., they are not from other sources used for the purpose of telling the tale.

I think they have possibly two purposes in the text. The first and obvious notion is that of verification—we all tend to believe in pictures more than we do in letters. Once you bring up a photograph in proof of something, then people generally tend to accept that, well, this must have been so. And certainly even the most implausible pictures in *The Emigrants* would seem to support that, the more implausible they are. For instance, the photograph of the narrator's great-uncle in Arab costume in Jerusalem in 1913 is an authentic photograph. It's not invented, it's not an accident, not one that was found and later inserted. So the photographs allow the narrator, as it were, to legitimize the story that he tells. I think this has always been a concern in realist fiction, and this is a form of realist fiction. In the nineteenth century, certainly in the German tradition, the author is always at pains to say, well, this is where I got it from, I found this manuscript on top of a cupboard in this or that town in such and such a house and so on and so forth, in order to give his whole approach an air of legitimacy.

The other function that I see is possibly that of arresting time. Fiction is an art form that moves in time, that is inclined towards the end, that works on a negative gradient, and it is very, very difficult in that particular form in the narrative to arrest the passage of time. And as we all know, this is what we like so much about certain forms of visual art—you stand in a museum and you look at one of those wonderful pictures somebody did in the sixteenth or the eighteenth century. You are taken out of time, and that is in a sense a form of redemption, if you can release yourself from the passage of time. And the photographs can also do this—they act like barriers or weirs which stem the flow. I think that is something that is positive, slowing down the speed of reading, as it were.

EW: One critic describes you as a ghost hunter. Do you see yourself that way?

WGS: Yes, I do. I think that's pretty precise. It's nothing ghoulish at all, just an odd sense that in some way the lives of people who are perhaps no longer here—and these can be relatives or people I vaguely knew, or writer colleagues from the past, or painters who worked in the sixteenth century—have an odd presence for me, simply through the fact that I may get interested in them. And when you get interested in someone, you invest a considerable amount of emotional energy and you begin to occupy this person's territory, after a fashion. You establish a presence in another life through emotional identification. And it doesn't matter how far back that is in time. This seems to be quite immaterial somehow. And if you only have a few scraps of information about a certain sixteenth-century painter, if you are sufficiently interested, it nevertheless allows you to be present in that life or to retrieve it into the present present, as it were.

One of the first things I wrote was a long prose poem [*After Nature*] about the early sixteenth-century painter Matthias Grünewald, about whom we know hardly anything at all apart from his pictures. And it's these lacunae of ignorance and the very few facts that we have that were sufficient somehow for me to move into this territory and to look around there and to feel, after a while, quite at home. It interests me considerably more than present day . . . I mean, going to Rio de Janeiro or to Sydney is something that I find entirely alien. You couldn't entice me there. The fact that I'm now in America seems extremely strange to me.

EW: One of your subjects in *The Emigrants* is a former school-teacher of yours named Paul Bereyter. What made you want to get beyond your own, as you put it, very fond memories and discover the story that you didn't know?

WGS: In the town in which I grew up—we moved when I was seven or eight years old from a village to the nearest small town—this is where I went to the primary school where I was taught by this particular teacher. And in this town throughout the postwar years when I grew up, between the ages of eight and eighteen, no one ever mentioned that this man had gone through years of persecution, had been ousted from his teaching post in 1935, and then had come back after 1945 to pick up the loose threads again. Everybody knew about it. A small town that had, I don't know, eight thousand inhabitants—everybody knew everybody else's business. The teacher himself of course—and that is the most perplexing aspect of that whole tale—never mentioned it either. And so clearly, as I was very attached to him as a boy—I admired this man greatly—I did want to find out the truth about it. And at that level you might describe it almost in the first instance as a piece of investigative journalism. Once you get hold of a thread you want to pull it out and you want to see, you know, what the colors of the pattern are. And the more difficult it gets—as it did in this case, because nobody in the town was prepared to talk to me about that life—the more intrigued you become, the more you know that there is something buried there. And the less you want to give up on it.

EW: Why wouldn't they to talk to you? This is forty, fifty years later.

WGS: Yes. Well, you know, the conspiracy of silence still lasts. It is something which people in other countries can scarcely imagine. It continues to puzzle me that when I grew up there, even when I was beginning to be capable of rational thought, as it were, at the age of sixteen or seventeen or so, this was scarcely fifteen years after the war. If I think back from the present moment in time, from 1997, sixteen or seventeen years back to 1980, it seems to me like yesterday. And so for my parents, for my teachers in 1960 or thereabouts, these calamitous years from 1941 to 1946, 1947, or so must have seemed like yesterday. And if you imagine that you have gone through such a dreadful phase of history, implicated in it in the most horrendous way, you might think that there might be an urge to talk about it. But I think that conspiracy of silence . . . it just came about, as it were. And it held, I think, even between married partners. I cannot imagine my parents, for instance, ever talking about these matters between themselves. It was just a taboo zone which you didn't enter. I think these self-generated taboo zones are always the most powerful ones.

EW: Because Bereyter was one-quarter Jewish he was not allowed to teach, he was rejected by the townspeople, he went to live abroad. But then he came back to Germany in 1939. Why?

WGS: I think there are quite good reasons for that, if you imagine the actual scenario. He must have been about twenty-two, twenty-three at the time. There is a photograph in the text which shows him with this family near Besançon on a Sunday afternoon, where he had gone to be a private tutor in a middle-class household after he had been ousted from his teaching post. He looks extremely thin and emaciated in that picture. One can conclude even just from that, that he must have been through what for him was quite a harrowing transition. Now, if you imagine France in the late 1930s and the young—what he was to all intents and purposes—a young German, partly Jewish schoolteacher sharing the dinner table of his employers every day, having taught the children in the morning, listening to the conversation around that dinner table, extended conversations as they tended to be in France . . . Midday meals would last for a couple of hours, and there would be plenty of opportunity for the paterfamilias to hold forth about his political views and opinions. And in French middle-class life I think the general inclination at the time was very much toward the right, i.e., the messages which came out of Germany through the news, through the radio, through the papers were very frequently endorsed: This is how you do it, this is what we should be doing. So by going to France, in a sense he didn't escape it. Ironically, all these things have come very much into the foreground over the last few weeks and months. Today in *The New York Times* you have a report about the Maurice Papon trial in Bordeaux. And this is all, as it were, connected with this particular tale.

So I think he must have felt quite an acute sense of discomfort in France. And of course by the late summer of 1939 one began to have an idea that, well, things were going to be very critical soon. So perhaps he did return to Germany because simply this was the place he knew best. And also I think, as the text makes clear at one or two points, he was very much in the German mold, this young teacher. An idealist coming out of the Wandervogel movement, as it were, a little bit like the young Wittgenstein when he went to upper Austria to teach the peasant children there, full of idealism, educational zeal, and so on. And this return to Germany in that sense is not altogether surprising.

The curious thing of course is that he was then drafted into the German army—as a three-quarter Aryan you were allowed, it was possible to serve in the army—and that he survived the whole war and did go back to the town where he had begun his career as a schoolteacher. That is to my mind the more puzzling side of this particular person's life: the return to Germany in 1945 or the staying there, and repressing, as it were, or being silent about all those dreadful things.

EW: And then even later, after he retired, Paul Bereyter went to Switzerland. But he kept a flat in that same town where at this point he loathed the people.

WGS: Yes, quite.

EW: Could you understand why?

WGS: Well, it's all in the nature of the double bind, isn't it? The psychologists know all about this. You want nothing more than to leave your parents, but you can't bring yourself to do it because you fear that they will despise you for leaving them alone. It's that sort of pattern. I mean, whatever you do is going to be wrong. And I think double binds govern to a greater or lesser extent almost all lives. Of course this is a particularly devastating form of double bind, if you are bound, as it were, to the nation that has done harm to you. But there are many Jewish-German stories which are exactly of that ilk.

EW: A friend of Bereyter's talks about "the contrarieties that are in our longings."

WGS: Yes. The history of Jewish-German assimilation, which goes back to the late eighteenth century, is full of this kind of ambivalence. Jewish names like Schiller and Lessing for instance—Jewish people took those on in admiration of the writers who they saw as the champions of enlightenment and tolerance. There was a very, very close identification between the Jewish population in Germany and the gentile population. And especially between the Jewish population and the country, the topography of the country, through their surnames. They were called Frankfurt or Hamburger or Wiener. They were, as it were, identified with these places. And it must have been extremely hard for them to abandon all this and to forget about it.

I'm essentially interested in cultural and social history, and the relationship between the Jewish minority in Germany and the larger population is one of the most central and most important chapters of German cultural history from the eighteenth century to the present day in one form or another. And if you have a wish to understand, as I did have quite early on, the cultural environment in which you're brought up, with all its flaws and terrible aspects, then there is no way past this issue. I talked before about the conspiracy of silence in, for instance, my hometown. And of course when I went up to university at the age of nineteen, I thought it might be different there. But it wasn't, not at all. The conspiracy of silence certainly dominated German universities throughout the 1960s.

At the same time of course, i.e., precisely at the time when I began to use my own brain, as it were, the great war crime trials, the Auschwitz trial in Frankfurt which lasted for many months, the Treblinka trial in Düsseldorf, and various other trials of this kind took place, and the problem for the first time for my generation became a very public one. It was in the newspapers every day, there were lengthy reports about court proceedings and so on. And so you had to contend with this. There was evidence of what had occurred, evidence in no uncertain terms. And yet at the time you were sitting in your seminars at university, you know, reading a piece of romantic fiction, E.T.A. Hoffmann or something, and never referring in any of those cases to the real historical background, to the social conditions, to the psychological complications caused by social conditions and so on. That is, what we were doing at university was pure and unadulterated philology, and this didn't get us any closer to what we wanted to know. Certainly for me it was always so. I think all children know this—if something is withheld from you, you want it all the more. And certainly from the age of eighteen or nineteen onwards, I was always, as it were, bent on trying to find out about these matters.

EW: Many of your family chose to emigrate to America, but you chose England eventually. Why?

WGS: In a historical accident. As a boy, my ambition was to go to America because America was the sort of ideal type country, at that time. But later on I had this, as it were, anti-American phase, which was part of growing up in Europe in the 1960s, where everything was very anti-American, and that must have cured me of my desire to go to America. When I was about twenty-one—this is round about the time when I left the European continent—I had no clear idea as to where I wanted to go. And Manchester, which is where I ended up, happened quite accidentally. I was looking for a job which would allow me to earn some money and continue my studies. I knew there were these language-assistant posts in British universities, and I wrote off to some of them and Manchester replied positively. So I packed my case and went there thinking that I might be there for a year or two or three until I got a doctorate and so on. But then eventually I got stuck in that country, because as it turned out, it's even nowadays a very pleasant country to live in.

EW: Although at one point, after studying in Manchester, you said you tried to live in Switzerland and also in Munich, and it didn't work. Why not?

WGS: The episode in Switzerland was in the German-speaking part, in a small town called Saint Galle. I taught at a private school there, which was run by some mafioso, you know, who got much more money from the students per month, or from one student per month, than he would pay a teacher. The whole setup was bizarre, and I knew from the first day I was there that I wouldn't do it for more than nine months, and this was what happened. Also the German part of Switzerland, beautiful though it is still—you do come across an enormous number of people who are terribly interfering. If you dig your garden on a Sunday, they'll come and denounce you to the police and say, he's digging his garden on a Sunday. I just cannot live with this kind of thing.

The year I spent in Munich and thereabouts I was working for a German cultural institute, the quite well-known Goethe-Institut. This was after I had taken my doctorate in England and I was looking for a career, and I thought I might do that. But as it turned out, I found it too officious, representing, however obliquely, Germany in a public sort of way abroad. I felt, when I saw it from closer up, that it wasn't me and that I'd rather go back and live in hiding, as it were.

EW: In hiding?

WGS: Well, where I am now is very much out in the sticks. It's in a small village near Norwich in the east of England. And I do feel that I'm better there than I am elsewhere in the center of things. I do like to be on the margins if possible.

EW: What attachment do you feel to Germany now?

WGS: Well, I know it's my country. Even after all those years. I've been out of it now for . . . it must be well over thirty years by now. Longer out of it than in it. Although of course I come from the edges, as it were, the southern edges of Germany— my granddad's house was on the Austrian border almost directly. I hardly knew Germany. When I left it I knew the territory where I had grown up and I knew Freiburg and I had been to Munich once or twice. But one didn't really travel terribly much in the midsixties or early sixties. And so I hardly knew it. I didn't know Frankfurt, I didn't know Hamburg, I didn't know anything in the north or the middle—Hanover, Berlin were all totally alien to me. So in a sense it's not my country. But because of its peculiar history and the bad dive that history took in this century or, to be more precise, from about 1870 onwards because of that, I feel you can't simply abdicate and say, well, it's nothing to do with me. I have inherited that backpack and I have to carry it whether I like it or not.

EW: And you still write in German.

WGS: And I still write in German, yes. There are very few writers who write in two languages, even people as accomplished as Nabokov in more than one language. Once Nabokov had moved across from Russian to English, he stayed in English. He still used Russian for translation purposes. But he didn't, as far as I know, write in that language after he had made the transition. Making the transition as Nabokov does, say, is a very, very risky and harrowing business. And so far I have tried to avoid making that decision. There aren't many other writers that I can think of who had to contend with that particular problem. There is Elias Canetti, who lived for many decades in London before he returned to Zurich, who spoke English perfectly well but never wrote a line in English, to the best of my knowledge. I think it is quite difficult to reach a level of sophisticated competence in a language. Even if you can babble on, it doesn't mean that you can write it well. That's quite a different proposal.

EW: Since you mention Vladimir Nabokov, there are references in *The Emigrants* to a man with a butterfly net, the boy with the butterfly net, Nabokov himself. Why does he hover over this book?

wgs: I think the idea came to me when I was thinking of writing the story of that painter. This particular story, as you know, contains among other things, as a secondary narrative, as it were, the childhood memoirs of the painter's mother. These are to quite a substantial extent authentic, based on authentic materials. I had the disjointed notes which that lady had written in the years between her son's emigration to England and her own deportation; she had about eighteen months to write these notes. As you know from the text, this family had lived in a small village in northern Bavaria, upper Franconia, called Steinach, then around 1900 moved to the nearest town, the spa town of Bad Kissingen. And if you read Nabokov's *Speak, Memory,* his autobiography, which to my mind is a wonderful book, there is an episode in it where he says that his family went to Bad Kissingen several times in exactly those years. So the temptation was very great to let these two exiles meet unbeknownst to each other in the story. And I also knew—and this is based on fact, it's not something that I artificially adjusted later on—that my great-uncle Ambros Adelwarth had interned himself in an asylum in Ithaca, which is where Nabokov taught for many years. And where, as one knows from his writings, he was always in his spare time going out with his butterfly net. So it seemed a very, very strange coincidence that two locations in the stories that I would have to write about were also Nabokov locations. Of course I also knew extremely well, from my time in the French part of Switzerland, the area around Lac Le Mans and Montreux and Vevey and Basel-Stadt and Lausanne. I knew all these places quite intimately. I didn't know of Nabokov, of course, when I was a student there; I hadn't got quite that far. I didn't know he lived there, and even if I had known, I wouldn't have dared to call on him, as you can imagine. But I knew the whole territory and I knew these lifts going up into the mountains that he talks about. And so it seemed an obvious thing to do and, again, an opportunity to create something which has a kind of haunting, spectral quality to it, something that appears, forms of apparitions of virtual presence that have, vanishing though they are, a certain intensity which can otherwise be not very easily achieved.

EW: I think one critic sees it as a sign of joy and another as foretelling death.

WGS: It's both, of course. People always want what seem to them to be symbolic elements in a text to have single meanings. But of course that isn't how symbols work. If they are any good at all they are usually multivalent. They are simply there to give you a sense that there must be something of significance here at that point, but what it is and what the significance is, is entirely a different matter.

I think that it was a question of trying to find, in a text of this kind, ways of expressing heightened sensations, as it were, in the form of symbols which are perhaps not obvious. But certainly the railway business, for instance. The railway played a very, very prominent part, as one knows, in the whole process of deportation. If you look at Claude Lanzmann's *Shoah* film, which to my mind is one of the most impressive documents of this whole fraught business, there are trains all the time, between each episode. They run along the tracks, you see the wagons, and you see the signals and you see railway lines in Poland and in the Czech Republic and in Austria and in Italy and in Belgium. The whole logistics of deportation was based on the logistics of the railway system. And I do pick that up at one point when I talk about my primary schoolteacher's obsession with the railways. So it seemed a fairly obvious thing to do. It always depends of course on how you put this into practice. The more obvious you make a symbol in a text, the less genuine, as it were, it becomes, so you have to try and do it very obliquely, so that the reader might read over it without really noticing it. You just try and set up certain reverberations in a text and the whole acquires significance that it might not otherwise have. And that is the same with other images in the text: the track, certainly, the smoke, and certainly the dust.

EW: Memory seems harder to escape the older that your subjects get. And most of them succumb, in a sense, through withdrawal or suicide. Why is memory so ineluctable and so destructive?

WGS: It's a question of specific weight, I think. The older you get, in a sense, the more you forget. That is certainly true. Vast tracts of your life sort of vanish in oblivion. But that which survives in your mind acquires a very considerable degree of density, a very high degree of specific weight. And of course once you are weighed down with these kinds of weight, it's not unlikely that they will sink you. Memories of that sort do have a tendency to encumber you emotionally.

EW: I'm thinking of your uncle Ambros, who suffered so acutely from his memories that he voluntarily submitted himself to shock treatment. And his psychiatrist describes how he wanted "an extinction as total and irreversible as possible of his capacity to think and remember." Why so extreme?

WGS: It's in many senses quite an extreme tale. What is hinted at in this story is that there was, between this Ambros Adelwarth and his employer's son, Cosmo Solomon, a relationship which went beyond the strictly professional, that they were to each other, to say the least, like brothers, possibly even like lovers. And that particular story and the way in which it unfolded in the grand years before the First World War went against the grain of history, across the fissures of history and contained within it at least something like a semblance of salvation. And you are permitted as a reader to imagine—the text never tells you to and never really makes it explicit—but you are permitted as a reader to imagine that these two young men, when they were together in Istanbul and down by the Dead Sea, lived through what for them were very blissful times. And it is the weight of that which brings him down, I think, in the end. You know, it's the old Dante notion that nothing is as horrendous as imagining the times of happiness from an environment which is that of hell.

EW: So many of your characters take such extreme action against memory. Is there any alternative? Is there any way to live with a memory? One of your characters, Max Ferber, says that while physical pain has a limit because eventually you'll lose consciousness, mental pain is without end.

WGS: Well, it is. There is a great deal of mental anguish in the world, and some of it we see and some of it we try to deal with. And it is increasing. I think the physical and the mental pain in a sense is increasing. If you imagine the amount of painkillers that are consumed, say, in the city of New York every year, you might be able to make a mountain out of it on which you could go skiing—you know, all the aspirin, powders. Of course we do see some of it, but people usually suffer in silence or in privacy. And certainly when it's a question of mental anguish, not all of it, only very little of it is ever revealed. We live, as it were, unaware; those of us who are spared this live unaware of the fact that there are these huge mental asylums everywhere and that there is a fluctuating part of the population which is forever wandering through them. It is a characteristic of our species, in evolutionary terms, that we are a species in despair, for a number of reasons. Because we have created an environment for us which isn't what it should be. And we're out of our depth all the time. We're living exactly on the borderline between the natural world from which we are being driven out, or we're driving ourselves out of it, and that other world which is generated by our brain cells. And so clearly that fault line runs right through our physical and emotional makeup. And probably where these tectonic plates rub against each other is where the sources of pain are. Memory is one of those phenomena. It's what qualifies us as emotional creatures, psychozootica or however one might describe them. And I think there is no way in which we can escape it. The only thing that you can do, and that most people seem to be able to do very successfully, is to subdue it. And if you can do that by, I don't know, playing baseball or watching football on television, then that's possibly a good thing, I don't know.

EW: What do you do?

WGS: I walk with the dog. But that doesn't really get me off the hook. And I have, in fact, not a great desire to be let off the hook. I think we have to try to stay upright through all that, if it's at all possible.

EW: Even as a young man, your uncle Ambros—you quote from his journal—says that memory seems to him like "a kind of dumbness," that it makes his head "heavy and giddy, as if one were not looking back down the receding perspectives of time but rather down on the earth from a great height." How does that work?

WGS: It's that sensation, if you turn the opera glass around . . . I think all children, when they're first given a field glass to look through, will try this experiment. You look through it the right way around, and you see magnified in front of you whatever you were looking at, and then you turn it round, and curiously, although it's further removed, the image seems much more precise. It's like looking down a well shaft. Looking in the past has always given me that vertiginous sense. It's the desire, almost, or the temptation that you might throw yourself into it, as it were, over the parapets and down. There is something terribly alluring to me about the past. I'm hardly interested in the future. I don't think it will hold many good things. But at least about the past you can have certain illusions.

EW: What are your illusions?

WGS: You do tend to think that the people who lived in New England in the late eighteenth century must have had a more agreeable life than nowadays. But then if you think about women having eight children and having to do all their washing in a bowl in the kitchen with a fire of sticks of wood, it's perhaps not quite as idyllic as one tends to imagine. So there is of course a degree of self-deception at work when you're looking at the past, even if you redesign it in terms of tragedy, because tragedy is still a pattern of order and an attempt to give meaning to something, to a life or to a series of lives. It's still, as it were, a positive way of looking at things. Whereas, in fact, it might just have been one damn thing after another with no sense to it at all.

EW: In *The Emigrants*, the painter in Manchester whom you call Max Ferber thinks he's found his destiny when he sees sooty Manchester with all its smokestacks, and he feels he's come there to "serve under the chimney." Why is he so drawn to dust? What does that mean for him?

WGS: We know the biblical phrase, dust to dust and ashes to ashes, so the allegorical significance of dust is clear. The other thing is that dust is a sign of silence somehow. And there are various references in other stories in the book to dusting and cleanliness. That of course has been in a sense a German and Jewish obsession, you know, keeping things kosher and clean. This is one of the things that those two in many ways quite closely allied nations shared. And there is the episode in the story of Adelwarth where the narrator goes through Deauville and a woman's hand appears through one of those closed shutters, scarcely open shutters, on the first floor and shakes out a duster.

There are some people who feel a sense of discomfort in tidy, well-kept, constantly looked-after houses. And I belong to those people. I've always felt it to be difficult to be in a house where this sort of cold order is maintained, the cold order which was typical of the middle-class salon which would only be opened once or twice a year for certain days like Christmas, perhaps, or an anniversary of one kind or another, and where the grand piano would stand in dead silence throughout the year and the furniture possibly be covered with dust sheets and so on. By contrast, if I get into a house where the dust has been allowed to settle, I do find that comforting somehow. I remember distinctly that around about the time when I wrote the particular passage that you are referring to, I visited a publisher in London. He lived in Kensington. He had still some business to attend to when I arrived, and his wife took me up to a sort of library room at the very top of this very tall, very large, terraced house. And the room was all full of books, and there was one chair. And there was dust everywhere; it had settled over many years on all those books, on the carpet, on the windowsill, and only from the door to the chair where you would sit down to read, there was a path, like a path through snow, as it were, you know, worn, where you could see that there wasn't any dust because occasionally somebody would walk up to that chair and sit down and read a book. And I have never spent a more peaceful quarter of an hour than sitting in that particular chair. It was that experience that brought home to me that dust has something very, very peaceful about it.

EW: One of the painter Max Ferber's techniques to achieve his goal of creating dust is to put on layers of paint and then scrape it off and then rub it out and put it on and scrape it off. And there's a point when you describe your own writing of this book where you seem to be adopting, almost, or finding yourself in the same position of writing and erasing and even questioning the whole, as you say, questionable business of writing.

WGS: Yes, it is a questionable business because it's intrusive. You do intrude into other people's lives, as I had to when I was trying to find out about these stories, and you don't know whether you're doing a good or a bad thing. It's a received wisdom that it's good to talk about traumas, but it's not always true. Especially if you are the instigator of making people remember, talk about their pasts and so on, you are not certain whether your intrusion into someone's life may not cause a degree of collateral damage which that person might otherwise have been spared. So there's an ethical problem there. And then the whole business of writing of course—you make things up, you smooth certain contradictory elements that you come across. The whole thing is fraught with vanity, with motives that you really don't understand yourself.

This form of creative writing, as it were, doesn't date back very far with me, but I have always been scribbling in one way or another. So it's a habitual thing. It's very closely linked, as far as I can tell, to neurotic disorders, that you *have* to do it for certain periods of time and then you *don't* do it for other periods of time, and then you *have* to do it again and you do it in an obsessive manner. It is a behavioral problem in one way. Of course it has other more positive aspects, but those are well known. What is less well known are these darker sides of it.

EW: I think at one point that someone says, referring to another text, that the book was heartbreaking but necessary work. It felt to me like that's what you were doing here, that this was heartbreaking but necessary work.

WGS: Well, I'm glad to hear that some people think that. I find that reassuring up to a point, but it's not going to allay all the misgivings that I have about it. And one of the most acute problems after a while is, of course, contending with the culture business that invariably then surrounds you, and you have to deal with it. Because when you do begin to write seriously, then it is very much like an escape route—you find yourself in some kind of compound, your professional life, and you start doing something about which nobody knows. You go into your potting shed . . . For me, when I wrote my first texts, it was a very, very private affair. I didn't read them to anybody, I have no writer friends and so on. So the privacy which that ensured for me was something that I treasured a great deal, and it isn't so now. So my instinct is now to abandon it all again until people have forgotten about it, and then perhaps I can regain that position where I can work again in my potting shed, undisturbed.

Who Is W. G. Sebald?

by Carole Angier

Who is W. G. Sebald? I had just read a book called *The Emigrants*, and that's all I wanted to know. *The Emigrants* contains four stories of exile from Germany. Each is longer and fuller than the last but still as coldly, heart-stoppingly clear, like a lake that keeps getting deeper and darker, but you can still see right down to the bottom. The first and last of the emigrants—the narrator learns slowly and painfully over many years—are Jews; the second is one-quarter Jewish. The third doesn't seem to be Jewish at all, yet his history is deeply interwoven with that of Jewish émigrés; in fact, in his story, the Jewish themes are strongest of all. *The Emigrants* is about many universal issues: time, memory, art, loss. But its main subject is the tragedy of the Jews and Germany.

It is one of the most hermetically sealed, yet one of the most open-ended works of art I have ever encountered. The four stories reflect each other like a hall of mirrors. Certain dates, like the summer of 1913, obsessively recur. There are beheadings in two stories and hermits in three. Most striking of all, Vladimir Nabokov appears in all four: sometimes as man, sometimes as boy, harbinger now of death and now of joy, but always carrying his butterfly net and evoking the great pursuit of his

Originally appeared in *The Jewish Quarterly*, Winter 1996–97.

autobiography, *Speak, Memory*. At the same time *The Emigrants* is fully, firmly grounded in reality. All four stories are illustrated with photographs from their subjects' albums. And large parts of the last two stories are taken up with extracts from people's diaries—which nonetheless contain some of the book's most beautiful writing and one of Nabokov's appearances.

What is going on? This is the opposite of a tricky, self-conscious, postmodern novel. It is exquisitely written; but it is modest and quiet and does not draw attention to itself at all. And yet this book raises the question of its own status more vividly, more directly, than any frivolous literary game. It doesn't matter historically. Only crazy people doubt the Holocaust happened, and puzzles about two or three survivors' stories cannot alter that. But if I have no historical questions about *The Emigrants*, I do have literary ones and personal ones. Is it fact or fiction? How did Vladimir Nabokov get into all the stories, even into Max Ferber's mother's diary? And who *is* W. G. Sebald?

It says on his door that he is professor of European Literature at the University of East Anglia. The man who opens it looks more English than German. He has also changed his name. It was Winfried Georg Maximilian; now it's Max. When we start to talk, however, a German intellectual—even a Munich intellectual—of the 1960s emerges: liberal, anticlerical, defining himself against the past. He still has his soft south German accent, too. I start by asking him about his antifascism, and in particular about his identification with the Jewish tragedy. How did that start? Not at home or at school, he says, with an ironic smile. Like all Germans of his generation, he was shown a film about the concentration camps at school, but hurriedly, without explanation. "I didn't know what to make of it at all."

W. G. SEBALD: I could easily say now that even as a boy I felt uncomfortable in that country. But whilst I was at school I didn't think about it. I had my mates, my girlfriends, I went swimming and riding in the summer . . . it took the first separation from home to change anything. When I went to the University of Freiburg to read German literature, I couldn't get anything out of the teachers there. It was totally impossible, because they all belonged to that generation. They'd all done their doctorates in the 1930s and 1940s. And of course they were all democrats. Except that it later emerged that they were all ardent supporters of the regime in one way or another. . . . There was something completely disingenuous about the whole setup of the humanities in the universities at that time, and I didn't like it at all. When I'd graduated, I remembered that there were such things as language assistantships in universities abroad. So I blindly applied to various places in this country and got my job in Manchester.

> IN MANCHESTER, Sebald ended up renting a room from D., a Jewish refugee from Munich. This was quite by accident—"I met his wife in a greengrocer's." Although she said, "You know, D. is actually from Munich," the two exiles never talked about what had made them both, in their different ways, leave Germany.

WGS: People like Peter Weiss and Wolfgang Hildesheim were starting to write then, and I was beginning to think about these things. And yet, when I was confronted by them in reality, it was a different matter. There was a sort of shyness, a sort of paralysis on both sides. It has taken all these twenty or thirty years for the paralysis to fade. In one sense I regret it, because

Withington and Didsbury were full of German and Austrian Jews, whom I could have talked to. But in another sense I don't, because I would certainly have said all the wrong things then. I think I might even say all the wrong things now.

HE SMILES—not his ironic smile, but an open, very charming one, and suddenly his face changes completely. I think that he still has the shyness and reserve he had with D., and that he mostly keeps his face a blank in case it, too, might say the wrong thing.

He studied Carl Sternheim for his M.A., and Alfred Döblin for his Ph.D., both writers with troubled relationships to their Jewishness. Later he taught Austrian literature—which is practically a history of assimilation, with writers like Hofmannsthal, Schnitzler, Karl Kraus. Of course. I'm not surprised that this shy, clever man should make this most difficult journey in books.

But I can't leave him there. Although I feel the same shyness, the same paralysis, come over me, I clear my throat and ask, "What about your family? They weren't madly opposed to the whole thing?"

WGS: Oh no, they weren't opposed. I come from a very conventional, Catholic, anti-Communist background. The kind of semi-working-class, petit bourgeois background typical of those who supported the fascist regime, who went into the war not just blindly, but with a degree of enthusiasm. They all fell up the ladder in no time at all, and until 1941 they all felt they were going to be lords of the world. Absolutely, there's no doubt about it, though nobody ever says it now. My father was in the Polish campaign, and he must have seen a thing or two. . . . His unit was camped out in the woods behind the Polish border, perhaps eight weeks before it all started. It's all in our family albums. The first photos have a boy-scout atmosphere—they're all sitting outside their tents mending their shirts, and underneath there are jokey captions like "Who needs women?" Then the order came, and they moved in. And now the photographs are of Polish villages instead, razed to the ground, with only the chimneys left standing. These photos seemed quite normal to me as a child. It was only later. . . . I only go home once a year, for two days, and I look at them now, and I think, "Good Lord, what *is* all this?"

CAROLE ANGIER: Can you talk to your parents about it?

WGS: Not really. Though my father is still alive, at eighty-five . . . it's the ones who have a conscience who die early, it grinds you down. The fascist supporters live forever. Or the passive resisters. That's what they all are now in their own minds. I always try to explain to my parents that there is no difference between passive resistance and passive collaboration—it's the same thing. But they cannot understand that.

CA: How do you feel about Germany now?

WGS: I still suffer from homesickness, of course. I take the train from Munich, and it turns the corner southwards, near Kempten, and I feel . . . and then as soon as I get out of the railway station I want to go back. I can't stand the sight of it. Nothing much has changed. They still have some pretty strange attitudes. You stand in Munich Pasing S-Bahn station at night, for instance, and some tramp rummages around in a bin. And some other chap who's just come from work goes up to him and says, "You don't do that here, you know. You ought to get a proper job." There's a lot of that about. And then there's all the rest of it.

I went to a Jewish cemetery not long ago, in a small town near Freiburg with a mill, straight out of the Brothers Grimm. There's this German forest and amongst it the Jewish graves. There's no one there, hardly anyone comes to visit. But at the bottom there's a camping site, where people come in the summer to grill their sausages and drink their beer. And there's a notice which says that visitors to the cemetery are not permitted to enter the camping site. Not the other way around.

> **WE LAUGH,** as there doesn't seem much else to do. Then he tells me about his previous book [*Vertigo*], in the last part of which the narrator returns to the village where he grew up "and remembers many things."

WGS: I thought I'd done it as discreetly as possible. But my mother was *mortified* to read details about families in our village. And ever since then she's never gone back. Wertach is here [he puts his cigarettes on the table], and here's Sonthofen [his matches]. There's a mountain between them [his coffee cup], and you have to travel around it. [He draws a semicircle around the mountain with his finger.] It takes forty-five minutes by bicycle.

Occasionally she meets someone from Wertach who's come to shop in Sonthofen, and if they don't mention anything she's reassured. She's like so many people in that country—the most important thing is that your neighbors mustn't think badly of you. There's nothing you could describe as civilian courage. It just isn't there. My mother couldn't say: "This is my son. He's now fifty-two years old, and he can do what he likes." That would be completely impossible for her.

HE CAN TELL ME THIS, I think, because his mother will never read *The Jewish Quarterly*. Or his father, or anyone else from Wertach or Sonthofen. The cemetery and the camping site are separate worlds in his life too; he alone moves between them.

CA: And yet, though you've lived in England for thirty years, you still write in German.

WGS: I hardly knew any English at all when I came to Britain, and I am not a very talented linguist. I still have quite bad days even now, when I feel that I am a barbaric stutterer. But that's not the main reason. I am attached to that language. And there's a further dimension, I think. If you have grown up in the kind of environment I grew up in, you can't put it aside just like that. In theory I could have had a British passport years ago. But I was born into a particular historical context, and I don't really have an option.

THE MOUNTAIN BETWEEN Wertach and Sonthofen has no coffee left in it, and outside, the gray Norfolk clouds have thinned. So we decide to talk about *The Emigrants* under the trees. The book is full of plants and trees. Nature is a second victim it celebrates, after the Jews.

WGS: *The Emigrants* started from a phone call I got from my mother, telling me that my schoolteacher in Sonthofen had committed suicide. This wasn't very long after Jean Améry's suicide, and I had been working on Améry. A sort of constellation emerged about this business of surviving and about the great time lag between the infliction of injustice and when it finally overwhelms you. I began to understand vaguely what this was all about, in the case of my schoolteacher. And that triggered all the other memories I had.

CA: So the schoolteacher in the second story, Paul Bereyter, and all the others, too, were real people? And these are their real stories?

WGS: Essentially, yes, with some small changes . . . Dr. Henry Selwyn, for instance, lived in that house, not in Hingham, but in another village in Norfolk. His wife was just like that, Swiss and very shrewd. She's still alive, I think, and so is Elaine, their most peculiar maid. Dr. Selwyn and his wife lived a smart county life for years. Terribly well spoken, he was, terribly well spoken . . . he told me about Grodno, sooner than I say in the story, but very cursorily. The first time I thought, *this is not a straight English gentleman*, was at a Christmas party they gave. There was this huge living room and a blazing fire, and one very incongruous lady. Dr. Selwyn introduced her as his sister from Tel Aviv. And of course then I knew.

CA: What about Dr. Selwyn's friend, the mountain guide Johannes Naegeli, and the extraordinary coincidence of your finding that article on a train, about the glacier releasing his body seventy-two years later? It's such a perfect image of the whole book—"And so they are ever returning to us, the dead."

WGS: Dr. Selwyn told me about his time in Switzerland before the First World War, about his friendship with a Swiss mountain guide, and how much it had meant to him. Later I couldn't recall the name he'd mentioned, or if he'd mentioned any name at all. Nor did he say that his friend had disappeared. But I did find that article on a train, just when I was starting to write the story. A mountain guide, in the same year, in the same place . . . It just needed a tiny little rapprochement to make it fit.

CA: Was Ambros Adelwarth, the subject of the third story, really your great-uncle?

WGS: Yes, absolutely. That wasn't his name, of course.

CA: What was behind Adelwarth's despair? Was it his homosexuality?

WGS: His story began with a photograph. When I was in the United States in 1981 I went to see my aunt, and we sat and looked at her photograph albums. You know how it is with family photos—usually you've seen them all before. But there's always one you haven't. And the photograph of Uncle Adelwarth in his Arab costume was one of those. I had known about this uncle, I'd met him as a boy, but he had never made any sense to me. Now, as soon as I saw that picture, I knew the whole story. . . . In a Catholic family that all gets repressed. It isn't even ignored—it's not seen, it doesn't exist. It doesn't fit in anywhere at all.

CA: There's also a diary in "Ambros Adelwarth," which is itself photographed. Did your great-uncle really keep a diary?

WGS: Yes, in several languages.

CA: I know. You can just make out one of the entries, and it's in English.

WGS: Ah. That, however, is falsification. I wrote it. What matters is all true. The big events—the schoolteacher putting his head on the railway line, for instance—you might think those were made up for dramatic effect. But on the contrary, they are all real. The invention comes in at the level of minor detail most of the time, to provide *l'effet du réel*.

CA: Or to provide a linking image, like the one of Nabokov?

WGS: I don't know that Ambros saw Nabokov in Ithaca, but it's entirely plausible. He lived there for ten or fifteen years. Everyone in Ithaca saw him at one time or another, with his butterfly net.

CA: But what about Max Ferber's mother meeting him in Bad Kissingen in 1910? Did you actually find that in her diary?

WGS: That's an episode from *Speak, Memory*. When I came across it I'd already read the memoir on which the diary is based, and in which there's a Sunday-afternoon excursion in the country. What you need is just a tiny little shift to make it match up. I think that's allowed. There are always elements that stray in from elsewhere. I take this to be a good sign. If you are traveling along a road and things come in from the sides to offer themselves, then you're going in the right direction. If nothing comes, you are barking up the wrong tree.

In the Paul Bereyter story, for example, there are echoes of

Wittgenstein in his period as a schoolteacher in Austria: the whistling, for instance, or, on the one hand, sacrificing himself to these peasant children and, on the other hand, feeling abhorrence for them. My schoolteacher did remind me of Wittgenstein; he had the same moral radicalism. But these details in the story come from Wittgenstein.

CA: And Ferber?

WGS: Ferber is actually based on two people. One is my Manchester landlord, D. The story of Ferber's escape from Munich in 1939 at the age of fifteen and of what subsequently happened to his parents is D.'s. The second model is a well-known artist.

HE SPEAKS AS QUIETLY as ever, but I suddenly feel slightly dizzy. "Which of the two, then," I ask, "is in the photo of Ferber as a boy?" He smiles, a combination of the ironic and the open, and says, "Neither."

"Ninety percent of the photographs are genuine," he adds quickly, like someone throwing a life belt to a drowning man. But that leaves 10 percent which aren't. . . . And what about the other "documents?" The message on Adelwarth's visiting card, for example—"Have gone to Ithaca"? He went to Ithaca, all right; but Sebald wrote that too. And Ambros's travel diary? Sebald wrote about half of it.

This is the answer to my question, then: *The Emigrants* is fiction. And the photographs and documents are part of the fiction. It's a sophisticated undertaking, and perhaps a dangerous one, given its subject. But I agree with Sebald that novelizing the Holocaust ("a quick chapter about Auschwitz, then back to the love interest again") is much worse. If literature can be made of this subject, it must be like this, solidly grounded in the real world. Besides, he himself has more doubts than anyone, which he expresses in Max Ferber. ("These scruples concerned not only the subject of my narrative, which I felt I could not do justice to, no matter what approach I tried, but also the entire questionable business of writing.")

So the reader does not need defending. He may feel a bit dizzy, like me, but that is a small price to pay for the elation of reading an extraordinary book. But I do have one doubt left: what about its models?

WGS: Yes, this whole business of usurping someone else's life bothers me. And of course I'm never certain I haven't committed errors of tact, of judgment, of style. . . . But—unless they're dead—I ask them. I show them what I've written before I publish it; and if anyone objects, I don't do it. In this way, for example, D. endorsed my use of his story and also of his aunt's autobiography, which he had given me, and which I used for Max Ferber's mother. In the case of the lady at Yverdon [who tells the narrator about the later years of Paul Bereyter], it was more complicated. It took me a long time to convince her that what I was up to was actually all right.

CA: Has anyone ever objected?

WGS: Yes, the artist who was the other model for Max Ferber did.

CA: But you still used him?

WGS: I changed his name from the German version, where it was quite close to the original, to something completely different. He doesn't want any publicity whatsoever, and I respect that. On the other hand, he is a public figure, and I got all my information about him from published sources, mostly from a huge tome about him by an American. If one is describing a creative process, one must be able to use material of this sort.

CA: It's the combining of the two stories that's the problem. I can just see people recognizing the artist and then believing that this is his life story forever after.

WGS: Exactly. So one has to be very careful.

I TRY TO PRESS HIM on this. But all he says is: "I think the vast majority of factual and personal detail that I use is very viable." At first I wonder if "viable" isn't a fudge word, used (perhaps unconsciously) to evade. But then I realize that he means it quite precisely. He simply isn't thinking any longer of the effect of his book on his models, no matter how hard I try to make him do so. He's just thinking of his book.

As we stroll back across the grass, I reflect that it could hardly be otherwise. If he didn't put his writing first, *The Emigrants* wouldn't be the great work of art it is. Curiously, the final proof of this for me is not a photograph, but the absence of one. The book ends with a description of three young women sitting at a carpet loom in the Lodz ghetto in *1940*, weaving literally (but as we know, in vain) to save their lives. I am convinced that I have seen their photograph on the last page; I remember the loom, their hands, their faces. But it isn't there.

A Poem of an Invisible Subject

by Michael Silverblatt

MICHAEL SILVERBLATT: I'm honored to have as my guest W. G. Sebald, the author of some of the most important prose writing of the century, including the novels *Vertigo, The Emigrants, The Rings of Saturn*, and now, *Austerlitz*. The prose has the breaths and cadences of poetry, and I wanted to begin by asking, were you influenced by German poetry?

W. G. SEBALD: No, not at all by German poetry. The influence came, if from anywhere, from nineteenth-century German prose writing, which also has prosodic rhythms that are very pronounced, where prose is more important than, say, social background or plot in any manifest sense. And this nineteenth-century German prose writing even at the time was very provincial. It never was received outside Germany to any extent worth mentioning. But it's always been very close to me, not least because the writers all hailed from the periphery of the German-speaking lands, where I also come from. Adelbert Stifter in Austria. Gottfried Keller in Switzerland. They are both absolutely wonderful writers who achieved a very, very high intensity in their prose. One can see that for them it's never a question of getting to the next

Bookworm interview, KCRW, Santa Monica, CA, December 6, 2001.

phase of the plot, but that they devote a great deal of care and attention to each individual page, very much the way a poet has to do.

What they all have in common is this precedence of the carefully composed page of prose over the mechanisms of the novel such as dominated fiction writing elsewhere, in France and in England, notably, at that time.

MS: When I started reading *The Emigrants* I was thrilled to encounter a kind of sentence that I had thought people had stopped being able to write, and I felt great relief at its gravity, its melancholy, but also its playfulness, its generosity. How did you find the way to reinvent such a sentence? It's not of this time.

WGS: It's not of this time. There are hypotactical syntax forms in these sentences which have been abandoned by practically all the writers now for reasons of convenience. Also because simply they are no longer accustomed to it. But if you dip into any form of eighteenth- or nineteenth-century discursive prose—the English essayists, for instance—these forms exist in previous ages of literature and they simply have fallen into disrepair.

MS: The wandering that the prose does, both syntactically and in terms of subjects, reminds me a bit of my favorite of the English essayists, de Quincey: the need, in a sense, to almost sleepwalk, somnambulate from one center of attention to another, and a feeling in the reader that one has hallucinated the connection between the parts. This I think is among the loveliest qualities, especially in the new book, *Austerlitz*.

WGS: Well, certainly, moving from one subject, from one theme, from one concern to another always requires some kind of sleight of hand.

MS: I was struck in the opening of *Austerlitz* by the way in which the narrator moves from a zoo, from the . . . what is it called?

WGS: The Nocturama.

MS: The Nocturama. It's a structure for animals that are awake only at night. And before long, the train station to which he returns becomes the double for the zoo. The eyes of certain thinkers become the doubles for the intense eyes of the nocturnal animals. Then the train station recalls a fortress, and there's a gradual opening out, an unfolding of structures and interpositions. The speaker might well be the person spoken to, by virtue of this logic. And it extends with, it seems to me, an invisible referent—that as we go from the zoo to the train station, from the train station to the fortress, from the fortress to the jail, to the insane asylum, that the missing term is the concentration camp . . .

WGS: Yes.

MS: And that always circling is this silent presence being left out but always gestured toward. Is that correct?

WGS: Yes. I mean, your description corresponds very much to my intentions. I've always felt that it was necessary above all to write about the history of persecution, of vilification of minorities, the attempt, well-nigh achieved, to eradicate a whole people. And I was, in pursuing these ideas, at the same time conscious that it's practically impossible to do this; to write about concentration camps in my view is practically impossible. So you need to find ways of convincing the reader that this is something on your mind but that you do not necessarily roll out, you know, on every other page. The reader needs to be prompted that the narrator has a conscience, that he is and has been perhaps for a long time engaged with these questions. And this is why the main scenes of horror are never directly addressed. I think it is sufficient to remind people, because we've all seen images, but these images militate against our capacity for discursive thinking, for reflecting upon these things. And also paralyze, as it were, our moral capacity. So the only way in which one can approach these things, in my view, is obliquely, tangentially, by reference rather than by direct confrontation.

MS: It seems to me, though, that in addition, it is the invisible subject as one reads the book and one watches moths dying or many of the images. It's almost as if this has become a poem of an invisible subject, all of whose images refer back to it, a metaphor that has no statement of its ground, only of its vehicle, as they used to say.

WGS: Yes, precisely. You know, there is in Virginia Woolf this— probably known better to you than to me—wonderful example of her description of a moth coming to its end on a window-pane somewhere in Sussex. This is a passage of some two pages only, I think, and it's written somewhere, chronologically speaking, between the battlefields of the Somme and the concentration camps erected by my compatriots. There's no reference made to the battlefields of the Somme in this passage, but one knows, as a reader of Virginia Woolf, that she was greatly perturbed by the First World War, by its aftermath, by the damage it did to people's souls, the souls of those who got away, and naturally of those who perished. So I think that a subject which at first glance seems quite far removed from the undeclared concern of a book can encapsulate that concern.

MS: I notice in the work, in particular in *The Rings of Saturn* and *Austerlitz*, the tradition of the walker. I'm thinking of Rousseau's *Reveries of a Solitary Walker* and thinking, too, that it was once beautifully common for a prose writer to write what he sees on his walk. In fact, the naturalist Louis Agassiz said that Thoreau sometimes used to bring things to him in the laboratory at Harvard, and that the things Thoreau picked up by accident were never less than unique. It was necessary for a writer to develop an eye. And it seems to my ear that the rhythms here have to do a great deal with the writing of entomologists and naturalists.

WGS: Yes, the study of nature in all its forms. The walker's approach to viewing nature is a phenomenological one and the scientist's approach is a much more incisive one, but they all belong together. And in my view, even today it is true that scientists very frequently write better than novelists. So I tend to read scientists by preference almost, and I've always found them a great source of inspiration. It doesn't matter particularly whether they're eighteenth-century scientists—Humboldt—or someone contemporary like Rupert Sheldrake. These are all very close to me, and people without whom I couldn't pursue my work.

MS: It seems that in *Austerlitz*, even more so than in the other books, there is a ghostly prose. Dust laden, mist laden, penetrated by odd and misdirecting lights . . . as if the attempt here is really to become lost in a fog.

WGS: Yes, well, these kinds of natural phenomena like fog, like mist, which render the environment and one's ability to see it almost impossible, have always interested me greatly. One of the great strokes of genius in standard nineteenth-century fiction, I always thought, was the fog in *Bleak House*. This ability to make of one natural phenomenon a thread that runs through a whole text and then kind of upholds this extended metaphor is something that I find very, very attractive in a writer.

MS: It seems to me that this book is truly the first to pay extended stylistic respects to the writer who, it's been said, has been your mentor and model, Thomas Bernhard. I wondered, was it after three books that one felt comfortable in creating a work that could be compared to the writing of a master and a mentor?

WGS: Yes, I was always, as it were, tempted to declare openly from quite early on my great debt of gratitude to Thomas Bernhard. But I was also conscious of the fact that one oughtn't to do that too openly, because then immediately one gets put in a drawer which says Thomas Bernhard, a follower of Thomas Bernhard, etc., and these labels never go away. Once one has them they stay with one. But nevertheless, it was necessary for me eventually to acknowledge his constant presence, as it were, by my side. What Thomas Bernhard did to postwar fiction writing in the German language was to bring to it a new radicality which didn't exist before, which wasn't compromised in any sense. Much of German prose fiction writing, of the fifties certainly, but of the sixties and seventies also, is severely compromised, morally compromised, and because of that, aesthetically frequently insufficient. And Thomas Bernhard was in quite a different league because he occupied a position which was absolute. Which had to do with the fact that he was mortally ill since late adolescence and knew that any day the knock could come at the door. And so he took the liberty which other writers shied away from taking. And what he achieved, I think, was also to move away from the standard pattern of the standard novel. He only tells you in his books what he heard from others. So he invented, as it were, a kind of periscopic form of narrative. You're always sure that what he tells you is related, at one remove, at two removes, at two or three. That appealed to me very much, because this notion of the omniscient narrator who pushes around the flats on the stage of the novel, you know, cranks things up on page three and moves them along on page four and one sees him constantly working behind the scenes, is something that I think one can't do very easily any longer. So Bernhard, single-handedly I think, invented a new form of narrating which appealed to me from the start.

MS: It's not only a new form of narrating. It's a new form of making things stop in space. Because the Bernhard works are often composed in one long paragraph, sometimes in one long sentence, if I'm not mistaken. The effect is of a dream, of being spoken to in a dream, and your attention can't help but flicker in and out. You can move back a page or two and discover the very careful links of the chain. But the intensity has been so nonstop that it's almost as if it breaks the mind's attempt to hold it in a chain.

WGS: Yes, it is that. Bernhard's mode of telling a tale is related to all manner of things, not least the theatrical monologue. In the early book that bears the English title *Gargoyles* and in German is called *Die Verstörung*, the whole of the second part is the monologue of the Prince of Salla, and it would make a wonderful piece on the stage. So it has the intensity, the presence that one can experience in the theater—he brings that to fiction.

MS: I've been very amused because critics of your work in America seem to be bewildered by its tone, and I don't, in fact, find its tone bewildering. I think they are unfamiliar with it because of its tenderness, a tenderness brought to bear on subjects that have usually compelled indignation, scorn, and, certainly in Beckett and in Bernhard, a huge and glittering kind of contempt or scorn. Here it really has that quality of—am I wrong here?—of infinite care taken in listening to speakers who are not being reviled in the slightest.

WGS: Yes. I don't know where it quite comes from, but I do like to listen to people who have been sidelined for one reason or another. Because in my experience once they begin to talk, they have things to tell you that you won't be able to get from anywhere else. And I felt that need of being able to listen to people telling me things from very early on, not least I think because I grew up in postwar Germany where there was—I say this quite often—something like a conspiracy of silence, i.e., your parents never told you anything about their experiences because there was at the very least a great deal of shame attached to these experiences. So one kept them under lock and seal. And I for one doubt that my mother and father, even amongst themselves, ever broached any of these subjects. There wasn't a written or spoken agreement about these things. It was a tacit agreement. It was something that was never touched on. So I've always . . . I've grown up feeling that there is some sort of emptiness somewhere that needs to be filled by accounts from witnesses one can trust. And once I started . . . I would never have encountered these witnesses if I hadn't left my native country at the age of twenty, because the people who could tell you the truth, or something at least approximating the truth, did not exist in that country any longer. But one could find them in Manchester and in Leeds or in North London or in Paris—in various places, Belgium and so on.

MS: I find it almost spooky how frequently these critics—I guess expecting the austerities and harshnesses of certain postwar prose—don't see that this is characterized by tenderness, bewilderment, horror, infinite pity, and a kind of almost willed self-mortification. That is, I am willing to hear and place great acts of attention on all things with the chance and hope that revelation will occur.

WGS: Well, I suppose if there is such a thing as a revelation, if there can be a moment in a text which is surrounded by something like *claritas*, *veritas*, and the other facets that qualify epiphanies, then it can be achieved only by actually going to certain places, by looking, by expending great amounts of time in actually exposing oneself to places that no one else goes to. These can be backyards in cities, they can be places like that fortress of Breendonk in *Austerlitz*. I had read about Breen-donk before, in connection with Jean Améry. But the difference is staggering, you know—whether you've just read about it or whether you actually go and spend several days in and around there to see what these things are actually like.

MS: It was once explained to me that there was in German prose something called *das Glück im Winkel*, happiness in a corner. I think that your radical contribution to prose is to bring the sensibility of tininess, miniaturization, to the enor-mity of the post-concentration camp world. So that a completely or newly forgotten prose tone is being brought into the postmodern century, and the extraordinary echo, the almost immediate abyss that opens between the prose and the subject, is what results. Automatically, ghosts, echoes, trance states—it's almost as if you are allowing the world to howl into the seashell of this prose style.

WGS: Well, I think [Walter] Benjamin at one point says that there is no point in exaggerating that which is already horrific. And from that, by extrapolation, one could conclude that per-haps in order to get the full measure of the horrific, one needs to remind the reader of beatific moments of life, because if you existed solely with your imagination in *le monde concentra-tionnaire*, then you would somehow not be able to sense it. And so it requires that contrast. The old-fashionedness of the dic-tion or of the narrative tone is therefore nothing to do with nostalgia for a better age that's gone past but is simply some-thing that, as it were, heightens the awareness of that which we have managed to engineer in this century.

A Chilly Extravagance

by Michael Hofmann

One of the most striking developments in English-language publishing in the past five years has been the extraordinary success of the books of W. G. Sebald. *The Emigrants, The Rings of Saturn*, and *Vertigo* were received—pretty unanimously, as far as I could tell—with deference and superlatives. This is the more unlikely as I don't think such a success could have been predicted for them or their author. Sebald, a professor at the University of East Anglia for many years and settled in England since 1970, nevertheless insisted on writing in his native German—and then taking a hand in the heavy, somewhat dated English presentation of his books. These books, furnished with, one presumed, the author's own photographs, hovered coquettishly on the verge of nonfiction; certainly, their elaboration of what appeared to be painstakingly researched historical narratives and circumstances contained much of their appeal. They called themselves novels, but they were more like introverted lectures, suites of digression, their form given them by the knowledge they contained; like water, finding its own levels everywhere, pooling and dribbling, with excurses on such things as silk, herrings, architecture, battles.

It was strange to see so many of England's hidden stops—

Originally appeared in *Arts and Books, Prospect*, September 20, 2001.

snobbery, gossip, melancholy, privileged information, eccentricities, the countryside reliably full of rich Keatsian glooms, daylight ghosts, dead machines, hulks of buildings, your Edward Thomas, your Pevsner, your Larkin, your Motion—so expertly manipulated by someone not even writing in English. But what was even stranger was that Sebald operated without any of the rigmarole or the pleasantnesses of the novel. The complete absence of humor, charm, grace, touch is startling— as startling as the fact that books written without them could enjoy any sort of success in England. Or, to take a different measure, that books without much pretense of character or action, but where the role of story is taken by thought or reading—or even more starkly, by the memory of thought or reading—could catch on at all. It is almost unaccountable to me that in the culture of "the good read" or "the book at bedtime" people would bother with books where the action—history—is always going on elsewhere, where the connection between the speaker and the hero or the plot is unspoken, unexamined, possibly nonexistent; where for the dearly loved cogs and springs of conventional fiction there is no greater lubricant or persuader than ruminant curiosity.

In *Austerlitz*, the unnamed first-person writer gives us his memories of encounters he has had with the eponymous Austerlitz, a figure who has obviously exercised considerable fascination over him: first in a station in Belgium, then in London, in Paris, and elsewhere. The encounters, the personality, the relationship are never particularly keenly seen; most of the book is made up of the divagations of Austerlitz's reported speech (a mode which in English is hard to distinguish over long stretches from ordinary narrative). Think of Thomas Bernhard's monologizing novels, but substitute repression for spill, airy scholarship for furious effect, and you have the general idea. Austerlitz's story—there seems to be pressure on Sebald to make it matter, as though his shimmering vitrines of facts are not enough by themselves—is that of a European Jew, born in Prague in 1934, put on one of the *Kindertransporte* in 1939, raised by a Welsh nonconformist minister and his wife, and later made aware of his origins and possible "identity," and finally consumed by them and by the thought of Terezin and Drancy, where his parents presumably met their deaths. The story, told in easy sequence, in meetings with ordered witnesses, is inevitably trite.

Sebald's writing has been more often praised than accurately described; the "beauty" so often reflexively attested to I frankly don't see. The dominant gesture is of something rigid in its peculiarity, or rigid in response to peculiarity. (The closest you get to drama in Sebald are certain moments of vaunting strangeness, promontories built out into the ectoplasmic sea in which the books have their being.) The sentences are grammatically complex and strictly correct. There is something paralyzed or immobilized about them. The manner is insouciantly, provocatively grandiloquent, neither sharp nor blunt. Inevitably, anything modern or contemporary distinctly threatens it: Canary Wharf appears anonymously as "sparkling glass towers"; one meeting between the narrator and Austerlitz is claimed, to the reader's utter disbelief, to take place in a McDonald's. It is a style that moves between stiff correctness, cliché ("white as a sheet") and jargon (boys at school who "hatched plots to extend their power bases"). A fire in an invalid's room has "yellowish smoke that rose from the glowing coals"—an impossibility, I would have thought—while moths flying round a lamp at night are seen "describing thousands of different arcs and spirals and loops"—where I would similarly query "different" as a bit of descriptive cant.

To me, Sebald's books have something gothic about them, a chilly extravagance, a numbed obsessiveness. Even their placidness and vagueness are gothic. On almost every page, I had the sense that I might have been reading Poe, or de L'Isle-Adam, or Hofmannsthal's Chandos letter, something learned and constrained and almost frightful: "Soon I would be overcome by this terrible anxiety in the midst of the simplest actions: tying my shoelaces, washing up tea-cups, waiting for the kettle to boil." At the same time, though, there is a complacency and lack of urgency in Sebald's academic sleuthing and the pedantic rosters of his prose catalogues that kept me from taking it as seriously as, say, Hofmannsthal.

Beyond that, the presence of descriptive tropes lifted straight from Kafka baffled me: the labyrinthine architecture of the Brussels Palace of Justice, ending in "dark cul-de-sacs with roll-top cupboards, lecterns, writing desks, office chairs and other items of furniture." Or the two messengers, "who were strikingly alike and had faces that seemed somehow indistinct, with flickering outlines, wore jackets furnished with assorted pleats, pockets, button facings and a belt, garments which looked especially versatile although it was not clear what purpose they served." Is Sebald using his novel to proclaim that Kafka was a realist? Or does he simply suspend his fiction for the occasional homage? Is he happy to be a postmodern pasticheur, to take the *Observer*'s praise for his originality, and run with it? Or has he merely gambled—probably correctly—that an English readership will be unfamiliar with the first page of *The Trial*, which goes on, in the new translation by Idris Parry, "a close-fitting black suit which was provided, in the manner of travelling outfits, with various pleats, pockets, buckles, buttons and a belt, and which consequently seemed eminently practical, though one could not be quite sure what its purpose was." It might have been different if the bit of Sebald's own writing that the Kafka has been fitted onto had amounted to anything, but the faces are just "somehow indistinct," in fact, they "seemed somehow indistinct." This is like nailing literature onto a homemade fog—or perhaps a nineteenth-century ready-made fog.

A Conversation with W. G. Sebald

by Joseph Cuomo

JOSEPH CUOMO: On the surface at least, *The Rings of Saturn* is a walking tour of the eastern coast of England. But all sorts of allusions and observations come in and out of the narrator's consciousness as he walks or looks out over a cliff or sits on his bed in a hotel room. And so we encounter with him any number of things, from the works of Sir Thomas Browne to Joseph Conrad to Borges to Swinburne to the life of the Empress Dowager. This description of the book is accurate, but it doesn't seem to describe what the novel actually does, what it accomplishes. And I think one of the difficulties we face in trying to describe the book is that in it you seem to have reinvented the narrative form. In fact, the narrative conceit of the novel seems virtually invisible, so much so that we are unaware of it as we read. There seems to be no artificial mechanism, no construct mediating between the reader and the experience of the page. A friend of mine, a very good writer, said to me that as soon as he had finished reading *The Rings of Saturn* he immediately started from the beginning again, because what had just happened to him—he couldn't figure out *how* it had happened. I was wondering how you approached this in the writing of it, the idea of narrative form. Was the structure a function largely of your unconscious associations during the writing process? Or was it something you plotted out in advance in a very deliberate way?

W. G. SEBALD: I can't quite remember how it worked. I had this idea of writing a few short pieces for the feuilletons of the German papers in order to pay for this extravagance of a fortnight's rambling tour. That was the plan. But then as you walk along, you find things. I think that's the advantage of walking. It's just one of the reasons why I do that a lot. You find things by the wayside or you buy a brochure written by a local historian, which is in a tiny little museum somewhere, which you would never find in London. And in that you find odd details which lead you somewhere else, and so it's a form of unsystematic searching, which of course for an academic is far from orthodoxy, because we're meant to do things systematically.

But I never liked doing things systematically. Not even my Ph.D. research was done systematically. It was always done in a random, haphazard fashion. And the more I got on, the more I felt that, really, one can find something only in that way, i.e., in the same way in which, say, a dog runs through a field. If you look at a dog following the advice of his nose, he traverses a patch of land in a completely unplottable manner. And he invariably finds what he's looking for. I think that, as I've always had dogs, I've learned from them how to do this. [Audience laughter.] And so you then have a small amount of material, and you accumulate things, and it grows; one thing takes you to another, and you make something out of these haphazardly assembled materials. And, as they have been assembled in this random fashion, you have to strain your imagination in order to create a connection between the two things. If you look for things that are like the things that you have looked for before, then, obviously, they'll connect up. But they'll only connect up in an obvious sort of way, which actually isn't, in terms of writing something new, very productive. So you have to take heterogeneous materials in order to get your mind to do something that it hasn't done before. That's how I thought about it. Then, of course, curiosity gets the better of you. For instance, this whole business about this atrocious Chinese civil war in the nineteenth century, which we know so little about in the West— I knew nothing about it—I'd found that remark in a tiny little booklet written, I think, in 1948, which was still there for sale, that this little local train which ran around there [over the River Blyth in England] had been destined originally for the court of the emperor of China, which was a very bizarre, erratic fact. And then of course you wonder which emperor, and you go to the Encyclopedia Britannica from 1911 and you rummage around there, and it goes on like this. Which is the most pleasurable part of the work, as you uncover these things and move from one astonishing thing to the other. The actual writing, of course, is a different story. That's far from a pleasant occupation. [Audience laughter.]

JC: This discovery process—the dog running in the field—is any of that happening while you're actually writing? You made a distinction between the two things, the searching and the reading . . .

WGS: Occasionally. I think when you write or do anything of

the sort, there are times when you almost know that you're on the right track. You don't quite believe it, but you feel more positive about what you're doing than at other times, and I think this is confirmed when things come in from the wings, you know, as you sit there, trying to straighten out a page. And, as it comes right, then quotations or figures or things that you hadn't thought of for eighteen years offer themselves all of a sudden. And I've always found that quite a good measure—that once things are going in a certain way that you can trust, then even in the writing process itself, things happen. For instance, the last part of this book [*The Rings of Saturn*] is all about silk, and that section, in turn, finishes with a number of pages on the culture of mourning. And on the very day when I finished these pages, I looked in, I think it was the *Times*, the daily circular, and there were all the events I needed. You know, the list of what had happened on a certain day 130 years ago or 220 years ago. And they all slotted into the text, as if I had been writing towards that point. It was quite amazing, but it does happen in that way occasionally—and that's very gratifying when it does.

JC: That process itself seems to be one that you describe in the novels: something inexplicable occurs; we don't really know what to make of it, but the fact that it does occur seems to carry enormous significance.

WGS: Yes, I think it's this whole business of coincidence, which is very prominent in my writing. I hope it's not obtrusive. But, you know, it certainly does come up in the first book, in *Vertigo*, a good deal. I don't particularly hold with parapsychological explanations of one kind or another, or with Jungian theories about the subject. I find it all rather tedious. But it seems to me simply an instance that illustrates that we somehow need to make sense of our nonsensical existence. And so you meet somebody who has the same birthday—the odds are one to 365, not actually all that amazing. But if you like the person, then immediately this takes on major significance. [Audience laughter.] And so we build. I think all our philosophical systems, all our systems of creed, all our constructions, even the technological ones, are built in that way, in order to make some sort of sense, which there isn't, as we all know. [Audience laughter.]

JC: One of the things that's so remarkable about the books is that you never try to use these coincidences toward some end, which is, I think, the point you're making: that we don't feel that we're being manipulated to see the world—I mean, in a lot of these pop-psychology novels there's a realization that, "Oh, because our birthdays are on the same day it means we *should* stay married." Or something like that. There's a tendency to reduce the world to some theme that this then becomes the proof of. And it's amazing to me that you resist that urge in novel after novel.

WGS: Well, it would trivialize it. Nevertheless, it has significance. The first section of *Vertigo* is about Stendhal, and this rather short piece finishes with Stendhal's death in a certain street in Paris, which is now called the Rue Danielle Casanova. I didn't know who Danielle Casanova was, except that Casanova meant something for me in the same context of that book, but not *Danielle* Casanova. The following summer I went to Corsica, walking through the mountains in Corsica, and I came to the coastal village of Piana, and there was a little

house with a plaque on it, and it was a memorial plaque for
Danielle Casanova, who had been murdered by my compatriots in Auschwitz. She'd been a dentist and a communist and
was in the French Resistance. And I went past the house three
or four times and it always seemed closed. Then on one occasion I went round the back and there was her sister. And then,
you know, I talked to her for a week. [Audience laughter.]
These things do happen. I have all her papers now, and I don't
know what I shall do with them, but . . . it's that sort of connection. And if that sort of thing happens to us, then we think,
perhaps, that not everything is quite futile. It gives one a sort
of passing sense of consolation, occasionally.

JC: We were talking backstage about your first book in German, *After Nature*, which is still in manuscript in English,
about how that book came about. You've been quoted as saying
that it was [the sixteenth-century painter Matthias] Grünewald
who brought you into it, but then you were telling me that it
was [Georg Wilhelm] Steller, who is in the second section, and
that that came out of a footnote.

WGS: Yes. It may be of interest because you don't know how I
got into this strange business of writing books of this kind. I
mean, I had never had any ambitions of becoming or being a
writer. But what I felt towards the middle point of my life was
that I was being hemmed in increasingly by the demands of my
job at the university, by the demands of various other things that
one has in one's life, and that I needed some way out. And that
coincided at the time—I just happened to be going down to
London and reading a book by a rather obscure German writer
called Konrad Bayer, who was one of the young surrealists, as it

were, postwar surrealists who'd been kept down by the famous Gruppe 47, and who subsequently took his own life. He'd only written a number of very slender little things, among them a book called *The Head of Vitus Bering*, and that had in it a footnote reference to an eighteenth-century German botanist and zoologist called Georg Wilhelm Steller, who happens to have the same initials that I have [audience laughter], and happened to have been born in a place which my mother visited when she was pregnant in 1943, when she was going from Bamberg, which is in the north of Bavaria, down to the Alps, where her parents were, because the bombers were coming in increasingly. She couldn't go through Nuremberg, which is the normal route, because Nuremberg had just been attacked that night and was all in flames. So she had to go around it. And she stayed in Windsheim, as that place is called, where a friend of hers had a house.

JC: Which is in the book.

WGS: Which is mentioned. This preoccupation with making something out of nothing, which is, after all, what writing is about, took me at that point. And what I liked about it was that if you just changed, as it were, the nature of your writing from academic monographs to something indefinable, then you had complete liberty; whereas, as you well know, as an academic, people constantly say, "Well, it's not correct, what you put there. It's not right." Now, it doesn't matter.

JC: There's a theme in your work that seems to be present from *After Nature* on. You've said,

We're living exactly on the borderline between the natural world from which we are being driven out, or we're driving ourselves out of it, and that other world which is generated by our brain cells. And so clearly that fault line runs right through our physical and emotional makeup. And probably where these tectonic plates rub against each other is where the sources of pain are. . . . And I think there is no way in which we can escape it. . . . I have, in fact, not a great desire to be let off the hook.

It seems that even in *After Nature*, particularly in Grünewald's painting *The Crucifixion*, that this theme is perceived:

> . . . the panic-stricken
> kink in the neck to be seen
> in all of Grünewald's subjects
> exposing the throat and often turning
> the face towards a blinding light
> is the extreme response of our bodies
> to the absence of balance in nature
> which blindly makes one experiment after another
> and like a senseless botcher undoes
> the thing it has only just achieved.

Was that idea, that theme, something that came to you in the writing of *After Nature*?

WGS: No, it's something that's preoccupied me for a long time. And I don't quite know why. But I think if you have grown up as I have done, in a village in the postwar years of the Alps where there weren't any cars or indeed any other machines worth speaking of, then you still know what silence is, you live in a house where the sounds are made by the house itself as it expands or contracts in the heat or the cold. You're not listening to the fridge going on and off all the time or the television in the other room or the central heating doing its thing. If you took a kind of closed-circuit camera film of, I don't know, a house here in Queens, you might well be excused if you got the idea that the people in it are only there to service the machines. [Audience laughter.] In terms of evolution, they are of the higher order, there's no doubt about it. Whether they are intelligent or not is neither here nor there, but they are of the higher order. They come after us. It is encapsulated in that wonderful image of the dog listening to the gramophone. There is that nagging sense that we're being kept, as it were, on sufferance. And I find the idea that perhaps one day a very severely decimated number of us might be kept like the dogs are now kept in New York not very appealing.

There was, as it were, a *décalage* or discontinuity in time so that in a sense in the late forties and early fifties in the Alps, you lived in the eighteenth century, for a few years. It's changed very rapidly. There was this unevenness of time. It's now very difficult to find any spaces where the twenty-first century isn't as yet. Certainly Germany has all been leveled out. Even in the 1960s, the frontier tracks in the east towards Czechoslovakia were, way back in time, underdeveloped, predeveloped. And that has all changed. So I think we move out of our earlier forms of existence or arrangements with nature at a price, always. There is always something we have to give up.

JC: Yes, I was feeling that today. I was typing up some of the notes here, and the computer program I was using was changing the letters. I would type a lowercase "a" because it was at the left margin of the poem, and the computer would change it to a capital. [Audience laughter.] I would go to the next line, and it would do the same thing.

WGS: Yes, my translator in the book that's coming out in the autumn [*Austerlitz*] has some Czech bits in it, which I found quite hard to write. At any rate, I haven't got a machine but the translator had a machine, and whenever she put those Czech bits in, the computer then put a one-and-a-half space for the next line, without explanation, without rhyme or reason. He's not answerable. This is the strange thing, that there's the same gap of incomprehension between us and these machines as there is between us and the animals we look at in the zoo. [Audience laughter.] There is a gap of incomprehension. We guess at what they might think about us, but we're not entirely sure.

JC: The fault line in your work seems to be the conflict between nature and civilization, and for you the fear is that nature is going to be destroyed. . . .

WGS: Well, in one sense, organic nature is going to vanish. We see it vanishing by the yard. It's not very difficult—I mean, you can hear the grass creak. Once you have an eye for it, if you go to the Mediterranean you can see that there used to be forests all along the Dalmatian coast. The whole of the Iberian Peninsula was wooded; you could walk from the Atlas Mountains to Cairo in the shade at the time of Scipio. It's been going on for a long time, it's not just now. There are pockets, Corsica, for instance, where you can see what these forests looked like. The trees were much taller. They were like the American trees, straight up, some sixty yards. But there are only pockets of it left. And you can see that it's a process of attrition that's gone on for a long time and that organic nature is being replaced through the agency of the psychozootic power, whatever one might call them, i.e., us—it's being replaced by something else, by chemistry, dust, and stones, which function in some form or other. And we don't know what it's going to be. On the whole, the thing evolves under its own steam. There's very little we can do to steer it.

JC: Of the four books which I know in English, *The Emigrants* seems to be the one that's least like the others in structure. There are four sections about four individuals, all of whom are more or less drawn from life. You've used the term "documentary fiction" to describe *The Emigrants*. I was wondering if that same description fits the other three novels at all.

WGS: Not really. They're all different. I think this one [*Austerlitz*] is much more in the form of an elegy, really, a long prose elegy. The first one, *Vertigo*, has very strong autobiographical elements, i.e., it looks at a period of disturbance in the narrator's life and tries to intimate how that might have come about. And it is also in the nature of crime fiction, in the sense that there are unresolved crimes. Which really happened—these gruesome murders in Italy which are described in that book—I mean, these are authentic elements.

JC: And the death of Schlag the hunter at the end of *Vertigo*?

WGS: That is also how it happened to me as I grew up in that village. But the image of the hunter is projected backward in the text in an illicit sort of way. So there are a few instances, certainly in the Stendhal and in the Kafka story, where some kind of legerdemain arranges things in a way suitable for the text.

JC: There is the effect in *Vertigo* when we read the last section—the narrator returning to his home town, W., which is also first the initial of your hometown—where we suddenly see what we've read before in a new light, and this turns around our perception of the earlier chapters. Was that something that came to you when you got to the last chapter?

WGS: No, that happens. For instance, as in psychoanalysis, when the narrative is finished, its beginnings show up in a new light. And in fact it happens with all forms of tales and stories, that the end really provides . . . I mean, after the tock comes the tick again.

JC: Was *The Emigrants*, then, very different from the other books, in the writing of it?

WGS: Different in the sense that *Vertigo* was very much a thing I did by myself, but with *The Emigrants* I had interlocutors, i.e., people whom I had known and was talking to, as it were, after their death, remembering who they were. Or people who, as in the case of the last story, were still alive. The last story is based on two figures, on a well-known contemporary painter and on a landlord I had in Manchester who was an émigré and came to Manchester in 1933; all the details about the childhood of his mother are from his mother. And this was for me quite a momentous experience, this whole Manchester business, because growing up in Germany you do perhaps learn the odd thing or did at the time . . . I mean, one didn't really talk about the Holocaust, as it is called, in the 1960s in schools, nor did your parents ever mention it, God forbid, and they didn't talk about it amongst themselves either. So this was a huge taboo zone. But then pressure eventually saw to it that in schools the subject would be raised. It was usually done in the form of documentary films which were shown to us without comment. So, you know, it was a sunny June afternoon, and you would see one of those liberation of Dachau or Belsen films, and then you would go and play football because you didn't really know what you should do with it.

Then later on when I started at the university in 1964, '65, for the first time these issues became public, in the sense that newspapers wrote about it a great deal. There was the Auschwitz trial in Frankfurt, which went on for a long period of time, well over a year, and where there were daily full-page reports about these things. And I remember reading those reports every day and being absolutely astonished at the details that came out of them. Nevertheless, despite my interest, unavoidable interest in these questions, I couldn't really imagine it at all; it was some form of abstraction; there were large numbers and you didn't know who these people really were. Because it is inconceivable of course in this country somehow that there is in the heart of Europe a country where there aren't any Jewish people. Or scarcely. There are some now, small growing communities again. In the 1960s you grew up there for twenty years and you never bumped into a Jewish person, so you didn't know who they were. Just some kind of phantom image of them. And so I go to Manchester. I didn't know anything about England nor about Manchester nor about its history or anything at all. And there they were all around me, because Manchester has a very large Jewish community, and very concentrated in certain suburbs, and the place where I lived was full of Jewish people. And my landlord was Jewish. I didn't talk to him about that nor did he talk to me about it either. We all avoided the subject. Until his wife, who was a good Englishwoman, once told me, well, do you know, Peter is actually from Munich? And I didn't know what I should do with this piece of information. But eventually, twenty years later, I went back and talked to him about it. And this is when all these things came out. And it turns out that as a small boy he was skiing in the same places where I went skiing. That somehow then sets you thinking. It's the reality of it. That he left traces in the snow on the same hills. These are different kinds of history lessons. They're not in the history books.

JC: When you were at university, I think you said somewhere that it was a very disturbing experience because most of the professors had gotten their jobs during the brown-shirt era, so there was a conspiracy of silence even there.

WGS: It's certainly true. I went to university in '63 from this place where I had grown up, which I had really never left before. I didn't really know Germany. At any rate, I went to Freiburg, which was pretty much the nearest place where you could study. And I had a sense of discomfort there all the time, but I didn't quite know why. It was simply that conditions for studying weren't very good, so I decided to go to Switzerland, where it was much easier to get into libraries and the numbers of students were smaller and so on. I really left Germany for practical reasons in the first instance. It's in retrospect that I seem to think—and I'm not entirely sure whether it's true—that I did have a sense of discomfort about the whole thing. The humanities were particularly compromised. The law profession as well, practically all . . . But certainly these people had all got their stars, as it were, in the thirties and forties. And if you then, as I have done subsequently, looked at what their Ph.D.'s were about, your hair stood on end. It really was a very unpleasant spectacle. Nobody mentioned it, but there was a very deeply ingrained authoritarianism, and as I have, I think, somewhere an anarchist streak in me, I couldn't really put up with that.

JC: Do you think that's why you didn't go back once you left?

WGS: There were a number of reasons, but that certainly was one of them. Because obviously once you had been in England for a number of years you could see a difference in attitude. Ideology didn't matter in England. You had colleagues who were extreme trade unionists and others who were Church of England all day long, and they all worked together and tolerated each other. But in Germany after the students' rebellion in the late sixties, early seventies, well, if you had leftish tendencies you could do a Ph.D. only in Frankfurt, Berlin, or Bremen. If you had liberal tendencies, you could do it pretty much anywhere. But this was it. You had to choose the train you wanted to be on.

JC: I want to talk about another subject that's in your writing, which is the moral difficulty of the writing process itself. In *The Rings of Saturn*, the narrator says,

> Janine had taken an intense personal interest in the scruples which dogged Flaubert's writing, that fear of the

false which, she said, sometimes kept him confined to his couch for weeks or months on end in the dread that he would never be able to write another word without compromising himself in the most grievous of ways.

It reminds me of something the narrator says about writing the account of Max Ferber in *The Emigrants*:

Often I could not get on for hours or days at a time, and not infrequently I unravelled what I had done, continuously tormented by scruples that were taking tighter hold and steadily paralyzing me. These scruples concerned not only the subject of my narrative, which I felt I could not do justice to, no matter what approach I tried, but also the entire questionable business of writing.

WGS: Well, yes, writing, as I said before . . . you make something out of nothing. It is a con trick.

JC: But there seems to be quite a preoccupation with making what is written true.

WGS: That's the paradox. You have this string of lies, and by this detour you arrive at a form of truth which is more precise, one hopes, than something which is strictly provable. That's the challenge. Whether it always works of course is quite another matter. And it's because of this paradoxical consolation that these scruples arise, I imagine, and that the self-paralysis, writer's block, all these kinds of things can set in. I had rather an awful time with this book that's going to come out [*Austerlitz*]. I don't know how many months I couldn't get . . . Normally on a good day I can do three pages handwritten, just about. But this, I never even got to the bottom of the first page. I started at seven in the morning till five in the evening. And you look at it. One day you think it's all right; you look at it the next day, it's awful. I had to resort to writing only on every other line so as to get to the bottom of one page. [Audience laughter.] I found that a very humiliating experience, but it did the trick in the end. But that's how it is. And it's very, very hard, I think, as most writers know; doubts set in, to keep one's nerve is difficult. Flaubert was in a sense the forerunner of writing scruples. I do believe that in the eighteenth century, say, Voltaire or Rousseau wrote much more naturally than people did from the nineteenth century onwards. Flaubert sensed this more than any other writer. If you look at Rousseau's letters, for instance, they're beautifully written. He dashed off twenty-three in a day if necessary, and they're all balanced, they're all beautiful prose. Flaubert's letters are already quite haphazard; they're no longer literary in that sense. He swears, he makes exclamations, sometimes they're very funny. But he was one of the first to realize that there was appearing in front of him some form of impasse. And I think nowadays it's getting increasingly difficult because writing is no longer a natural thing for us.

Flaubert said at one point something like, "*L'art est un luxe. Il faut des mains calmes et blanches.*" And then he went on to say something like, "*On fait d'abord une concession et puis deux et puis on sent fou complètement.*" [Audience laughter.] And that's very true: you make one concession, you make another one, and in the end, nothing matters anymore.

JC: I was wondering if what the narrator in *The Emigrants* says in the Paul Bereyter section had some bearing when you were writing *Austerlitz*:

> I imagined him, stretched out on the track [where he committed suicide]. . . . Such endeavors to imagine his life and death did not, as I had to admit, bring me any closer to Paul, except at best for brief emotional moments of the kind that seem presumptuous to me. It is in order to avoid this sort of wrongful trespass that I have written down what I know of Paul Bereyter.

He was a teacher of yours.

WGS: Yes, a primary-school teacher.

JC: And *Austerlitz* is dealing with a similar subject as in *The Emigrants*: a man, Jacques Austerlitz, left Czechoslovakia in 1939 as a young boy, and then he doesn't remember most of what had happened until he's at a more advanced age. First of all, was this someone that you did know, as in *The Emigrants*?

WGS: The Austerlitz character has two models and bits from other lives also. There was a colleague of mine, a distant colleague in London—London is a hundred miles from Norwich, but I had some contacts there—and I had bumped into this man a number of times fortuitously, in Belgium of all places, in the late 1960s, in unlikely places. He was an architectural historian, somewhat older than me, about ten, twelve years older, a born, very gifted teacher. And whenever we met I just listened to him. Before I came to England I hadn't had any teachers apart from this primary schoolteacher who I wanted to listen to. And this chap was interested in the architecture of the capitalist era—opera houses, railway stations, that sort of thing—and he could go on endlessly about the most fascinating details. Then I lost sight of him for a while, and in the 1990s we made contact again. So this is one foil of the story.

But there is another foil, which is the life story of a woman, and that story I came across, as one does sometimes, on television. You know how ephemeral these appearances are on television—you see a film or you don't see it, and then it vanishes forever and you can't get a copy of it despite your best efforts. But there was this story of a woman who together with her twin sister had also come to Britain on one of these *Kindertransporte*, as they were called, trains with very young children leaving Germany or Czechoslovakia or Austria just before the outbreak of war. And those two girls were, I think, two-and-a-half to three years old. They came out of a Jewish Munich orphanage and they were fostered by a Welsh fundamentalist childless couple who then went on to erase their identity. And both foster parents ended tragically, as one might say, the father in a lunatic asylum, the mother through an early death. And so the children never really knew who they were. This is just one strand, as it were, of the story which I then put together with that other life history.

JC: I was wondering if that fear of presumption is what was so inhibiting in the writing of *Austerlitz*.

WGS: Well, it's always there. I think certainly for a German gentile to write about Jewish lives is not unproblematic. There are examples of that, writers attempting this in Germany in the

1960s and 70s, and many of these attempts are—one can't say it really otherwise—shameful. In the sense that they usurp the lives of these people. Perhaps not consciously so; they might be done with the best of intentions, but in the making it comes so that it isn't right, morally not right. That is, something is spun out of the lives of these victims which is gratifying for the author or for the author's audience. It's very, very difficult terrain. I don't know whether I succeed in this, but I was certainly conscious from the beginning that even in talking to the people who you perhaps might want to portray, there are thresholds which you cannot cross, where you have to keep your distance. It's difficult and every case is different. Yet at the same time, of course, the likes of us ought to try to say how they receive these stories. But there isn't a self-evident way of going about it. It's a more acute variation of a problem that all writers have. So one has to be very careful.

JC: You've said that *After Nature* was very freeing because you could do it more or less by yourself. Were *Vertigo* and *The Rings of Saturn* also free writing experiences?

WGS: Certainly with *Vertigo* I had hardly any trouble at all. The last section of it, I wrote in very agreeable surroundings without consulting anything particularly, just wrote it down. But as I go along it seems to get more difficult. And pretty much in the same measure. *The Emigrants* was more difficult than this, and the last one I could hardly do, so I dread to think what the next one will be like. [Audience laughter.] I'll have to wait and see. But it's not like being a solicitor or a surgeon, you know: if you have taken out 125 appendixes, then the 126th one you can do in your sleep. With writing it's the other way around.

JC: One thing we've discussed a couple of times, which is in *The Rings of Saturn,* is the degree to which the writing process is self-contained or illusionary for the writer as well as for the audience. Michael Hamburger and the narrator—Michael Hamburger also happens to be the translator for *After Nature* and he's in *The Rings of Saturn* as a character—Michael Hamburger and the narrator are discussing the writing process. From the novel:

> For days and weeks on end one racks one's brains to no avail, and, if asked, one could not say whether one goes on writing purely out of habit, or a craving for admiration, or because one knows not how to do anything other, or out of sheer wonderment, despair or outrage, any more than one could say whether writing renders one more perceptive or more insane. Perhaps we all lose our sense of reality to the precise degree to which we are engrossed in our own work, and perhaps that is why we see in the increasing complexity of our mental constructs a means for greater understanding, even while intuitively we know that we shall never be able to fathom the imponderables that govern our course through life.

This seems to be a theme that's all over your work, which is that the part of the world that we know is minuscule. And the part of the world that we don't know is enormous. Yet within the part that we do know—there's such a great deal of agonizing in your work over getting that part right and getting the voice true. And yet, it may be that we're trying to do this just to convince ourselves that we do know something about the world after all.

WGS: I think that's pretty much how it is. You can't always see, I think, the reality of what we're doing in the pathological variant, because all modes of behavior have pathological variants. And writing and creating something is about elaboration. You have a few elements. You build something. You elaborate until you have something that looks like something. And elaboration is, of course, the vice of paranoia. If you read texts written by paranoiacs, they're syntactically correct, the orthography is all right, but the content is insane, because they start from a series of axioms which are out of synch. But the degree of elaboration is absolutely fantastic. It goes on and on and on and on. You can see from that that the degree of elaboration is not the measure of truth. And that is exactly the same problem because, certainly in prose fiction, you have to elaborate. You have one image and you have to make something of it—half a page, or three-quarters, or one-and-a-half—and it only works through linguistic or imaginative elaboration. Of course you might well think, as you do this, that you are directing some form of sham reality.

JC: Two more things I want to get into before we close. One is—and this is that same theme again—in *The Rings of Saturn*:

> The invisibility and intangibility of that which moves us remained an unfathomable mystery for Thomas Browne too, who saw our world as no more than a shadow image of another one far beyond. . . . And yet, says Browne, all knowledge is enveloped in darkness. What we perceive are no more than isolated lights in the abyss of ignorance, in the shadow-filled edifice of the world. We study the order of things, says Browne, but we cannot grasp their innermost essence.

There's something in that quote which reminds me of a passage from *The Brothers Karamazov*, Father Zossima saying,

> Many things on earth are hidden from us . . . and the roots of our thoughts and feelings are not here but in other worlds. That is why philosophers say that it is impossible to comprehend the essential nature of things on earth . . . what grows lives and is alive only through the feeling of its contact with other mysterious worlds. . . .

One other connection would be to the work of Czeslaw Milosz, Adam Zagajewski, and Joseph Brodsky. Do you see yourself as writing in a similar vein, thematically?

WGS: Well, what I think some of these people have in common is an interest in metaphysics. Certainly in Dostoyevsky this is evident. I think the best sections in Dostoyevsky's writings are those which are metaphysical rather than religious. And metaphysics is something that's always interested me, in the sense that one wants to speculate about these areas that are beyond one's ken, as it were. I've always thought it very regrettable and, in a sense, also foolish, that the philosophers decided somewhere in the nineteenth century that metaphysics wasn't a respectable discipline and had to be thrown overboard, and reduced themselves to becoming logicians and statisticians. It seemed a very poor diet, somehow, to me.

So metaphysics, I think, is a legitimate concern. Writers like Kafka, for instance, are interested in metaphysics. If you read a story like "The Investigations of a Dog," it has a subject whose epistemological horizon is very low. He doesn't realize anything above the height of one foot. He makes incantations so that the bread comes down from the dinner table. How it comes down, he doesn't know. But he knows that if he performs certain rites, then certain events will follow. And then he goes, this dog, through the most extravagant speculations about reality, which we know is quite different. As he, the dog, has this limited capacity of understanding, so do we. And so it's quite legitimate to ask—and of course it can become a parlor game, as it did in Bloomsbury—these philosophers said, "Are we sure that we're really sitting here at this table?"

JC: I haven't asked you about the photographs in the books. Two things occur to me. In *The Emigrants,* you've said, I think, that 90 percent of the photographs are authentic. But there's a passage in *Vertigo,* speaking of Kafka, where the narrator is on a bus and he encounters two twin boys who look exactly like Franz Kafka did at that age. He's traveling to a place where Kafka had spent some time, and he wants to get a photograph of these two boys. He asks the parents of the boys to send him a photograph, without giving their names, just because he needs to have this photograph. Of course the parents think that he's a pederast and don't want to have anything to do with him. But then the passage ends, "I remained motionless on that bus seat from then on, embarrassed to the utmost degree and consumed with an impotent rage at the fact that I would now have no evidence whatsoever to document this most improbable coincidence." I was wondering if this was another form of documentation—for the photographs in the books to document coincidence itself.

WGS: Well, that particular episode actually happened as it is described, and it was from that time onwards that I always have one of those small cameras in my pocket. [Audience laughter.] It was a completely unnerving afternoon. It was really terrible. But, you know, it does happen. Doubles do exist. The irony is, of course, that Kafka's prose fiction is full of twins or triplets. And that it should happen in real life seemed to me quite implausible. I mean, sometimes one asks oneself later on whether one's made it up or not. And it's not always quite clear.

JC: The last question is, again, about coincidence. I was wondering, going back to the theme that we discussed earlier on, the fault line between nature and civilization, if you feel sometimes that coincidence or duplication is a way in which nature is breaking through the surface of our civilized lives. We may not know what it means, but we have a sense that something beyond us is taking place.

WGS: Well, I don't think I could speculate about this, but one sometimes does have a sense that there is a double floor someplace, or that events are outside your control. This notion of the autonomous individual who is in charge of his or her fate is one that I couldn't really subscribe to. Certainly my own life experience is that always when I thought I had things sorted out and I was in control, the next day something happened which completely undid everything I had wanted to do. And so it goes on. The illusion that I had some control over my life goes up to about my thirty-fifth birthday and then it stopped. [Audience laughter.] Now I'm out of control.

Rings of Smoke

by Ruth Franklin

I

If there is an underworld where the darkest nightmares of the twentieth century dwell, W. G. Sebald could be its Charon. Starting with *Vertigo*, which combines sketches of Kafka and Stendhal with a fictionalized record of travels in Italy and elsewhere, and ending with *Austerlitz*, the story of a boy sent to England via *Kindertransporte* in 1939 and brought up under a false name, all of Sebald's books have been about bridging gaps and about the impossibility of bridging gaps—between memory and forgetting, between art and reality, between the living and the dead. These extraordinary works are different on each reading, constantly in flux. Sebald's sudden death in a car accident last December was tragic for many reasons, but for his readers foremost because his books, all of them variations on a small group of themes, seemed parts of a whole that had not yet been brought to completion but had already broken new literary ground.

Like the origami figures that open and close with a twist of the fingers, Sebald's prose moves simultaneously inward and outward. The opening of *Austerlitz* is exemplary:

Originally appeared in *The New Republic*, September 23, 2002. Reprinted by permission of *The New Republic*, © 2002, The New Republic, LLC.

In the second half of the 1960s I traveled repeatedly from England to Belgium, partly for study purposes, partly for other reasons which were never entirely clear to me, staying sometimes for just one or two days, sometimes for several weeks.

On one of these Belgian excursions which, as it seemed to me, always took me further and further abroad, I came on a glorious early summer's day to the city of Antwerp, known to me previously only by name. Even on my arrival, as the train rolled slowly over the viaduct with its curious pointed turrets on both sides and into the dark station concourse, I had begun to feel unwell, and this sense of indisposition persisted for the whole of my visit to Belgium on that occasion. I still remember the uncertainty of my footsteps as I walked all round the inner city, down Jeruzalemstraat, Nachtegaalstraat, Pelikaanstraat, Paradijsstraat, Immerseelstraat, and many other streets and alleyways, until at last, plagued by a headache and my uneasy thoughts, I took refuge in the zoo by the Astridplein, next to the Centraal Station, waiting for the pain to subside. I sat there on a bench in dappled shade, beside an aviary full of brightly feathered finches and siskins fluttering about. As the afternoon drew to a close I walked through the park, and finally went to see the Nocturama, which had first been opened only a few months earlier. It was some time before my eyes became used to its artificial dusk and I could make out different animals leading their sombrous lives behind the glass by the light of a pale moon. I cannot now recall exactly what creatures I saw on that visit to the Antwerp Nocturama, but there were probably bats and jerboas from Egypt and the Gobi Desert, native European hedgehogs and owls, Australian opossums, pine martens, dormice, and lemurs, leaping from branch to branch, darting back and forth over the grayish-yellow sandy ground, or disappearing into a bamboo thicket. The only animal which has remained lingering in my memory is the raccoon. I watched it for a long time as it sat beside a little stream with a serious expression on its face, washing the same piece of apple over and over again, as if it hoped that all this washing, which went beyond any reasonable thoroughness, would help it to escape the unreal world in which it had arrived, so to speak, through no fault of its own.

The single-mindedness with which this passage proceeds is Sebald's signature. Each sentence, bizarre or mundane, contributes another piece to the overall structure until that structure seems unable to sustain any more weight. The straightforward remark that opens the book, about the trips to and from Belgium, is immediately complicated. What are these reasons that were never clear to the speaker? How can these "excursions," all within the country, take him "further and further abroad"? The next sentences deepen the mystery: the narrator's sudden illness, the fantastic street names— Jerusalem, Nightingale, Pelican, Paradise, and, most evocatively, Eternal Soul—and finally the Nocturama itself, a symbol so potent that, like all of Sebald's symbols, it stops just this side of parody. And here, too, we get a final shrug of contradiction: Sebald claims to have difficulty remembering which animals he saw in the Nocturama, but at the same time he offers an almost comically specific series of examples. The tug-of-war between what is and what cannot be never stops.

The world of Sebald's books is its own Nocturama, inhabited by creatures at home in the dark. Like the raccoon that he describes so plaintively, Sebald's characters emerge with sudden clarity from the haze of their surroundings, obsessively repeating whatever action they have chosen, though it will not bring them the escape for which they so desperately yearn. They are destroyed souls, fractured under the burden of the pain that they bear. There is the tortured Kafka in *Vertigo*, sick and disoriented while traveling in Austria and Italy, tormented by dreams "in which everything was forever splitting and multiplying, over and again, in the most terrifying manner." There is the painter Max Ferber in *The Emigrants*, a Jew sent to England as a child during the war, whose parents died in Dachau: "That tragedy in my youth struck such deep roots within me that it later shot up again, put forth evil flowers, and spread the poisonous canopy over me which has kept me so much in the shade and dark in recent years." There is the Ashbury family in *The Rings of Saturn*, who embroider cloth all day and undo their work each night, and feel that "we never got used to being on this earth and life is just one great, ongoing incomprehensible blunder." And there is Jacques Austerlitz, whose life journey is driven by a blind and unsatisfiable longing to recapture the childhood memories he has entirely, unwillingly suppressed.

The strangest thing about Sebald's incomparably strange work is that upon first reading it gives us no reason to think that it is fiction. Though *Austerlitz* was largely taken as a novel, Sebald himself refused to designate it as such; in an interview he called it "a prose book of indefinite form." Indeed, why must the passage above be anything other than notes from an idiosyncratic travel journal? The street names, improbable though they may be, are easily verified with a map of Antwerp, and the zoo, located near the central train station just as he says, does in fact have a Nocturama. But though the books are marked by an extraordinary profusion of facts—snippets from Kafka's letters, notes on the mating practices of herrings, even reproductions of train tickets and restaurant receipts that appear to document the narrator's journeys—fiction pulls at them with the force of gravity. The four stories that constitute *The Emigrants* are connected by a single image that flits through each of them: the figure of Nabokov with his butterfly net, sometimes a grown man, sometimes a boy. And the four sketches of *Vertigo* each contain a line from a story by Kafka, slightly rephrased on each repetition, describing a corpse lying beneath a cloth on a bier. The improbability of all four characters in *The Emigrants* crossing paths with Nabokov and the impossibility of a manifestation of Kafka's image appearing in all four parts of *Vertigo* is but one signal of the turn into fiction. As one reads more deeply into Sebald's work, its fictionality becomes utterly essential.

But while fiction tugs at one sleeve, reality tugs at the other with nearly equal force, most dramatically in the black-and-white photographs that Sebald has strewn about all his prose books. The photographs have neither captions nor credits to give a clue to their provenance; the text describes the taking of some of them, while others seem to be more generally illustrative, and still others entirely random. In the last chapter of *Vertigo*, for instance, the narrator, visiting his hometown after many years of absence, mentions a photo album that his father gave his mother as a Christmas present during the first year of the war.

> In it are pictures of the Polish campaign, all neatly captioned in white ink. Some of these photographs show gypsies who had been rounded up and put in detention. They are looking out, smiling, from behind the barbed wire, somewhere in a far corner of the Slovakia where my father and his vehicle repairs unit had been stationed for several weeks before the outbreak of war.

We are then shown a photograph of a woman carrying a baby in a bundle, dressed in Gypsy-like clothes, behind a wire fence, with the caption "Zigeuner" (the German word for Gypsy) in white ink. But for every photograph such as this one, there is another that firmly denies any easy correspondence with the text. Several pages earlier Sebald mentions an iron memorial cross that stands in the town graveyard to commemorate four young soldiers who died in a "last skirmish" in April 1945, and he lists their names. When we turn the page there is the cross; but it looks as if there are five names on it, not four, and the photograph is too blurry to make out any names.

The conflict between fact and fiction reaches its epitome in the voice that narrates all these stories of loss. Sebald seems to encourage us to think of this persona as something like his own. His narrator (the books share a single voice) occasionally offers biographical details that are identical to Sebald's own life: he is married, he lives in East Anglia, he was born toward the end of World War II in an Alpine German town, and came to England in the 1960s. Yet these details, like the photographs, obscure as much as they reveal. There are moments of startling intimacy, but even as Sebald's narrator seems to bare his soul, he tells us nothing about himself. And he favors a particularly disorienting narrative device: most of Sebald's characters tell their stories through direct encounters with the narrator, in monologues. At a crucial moment in some of the monologues, Sebald will switch from third person to first person, so that the narrator vanishes, leaving the character behind. Since he does not use quotation marks, the shift is seamless. This is not an "unreliable narrator," it is an unreliable narrative.

But even as Sebald builds layer upon layer of disguise, his books stumble over their own sentences in their desire to explain themselves to the reader, as the crushing pile of symbols in the opening to *Austerlitz* illustrates. The books search for patterns in nature and in human life, and as they do so they obsessively repeat themselves. To take one instance: *The Rings of Saturn* begins with a quotation from an encyclopedia that describes the planet's rings as "consist[ing] of ice crystals and probably meteorite particles describing circular orbits around the planet's equator. In all likelihood these are fragments of a former moon that was too close to the planet and was destroyed by its tidal effect." The circular motif is repeated throughout the book, in everything from the déjà vu the narrator experiences visiting a friend's apartment to an extraordinary vision that is one of Sebald's most beautiful and mystical moments: "At earlier times, in the summer evenings during my childhood when I had watched from the valley as swallows circled in the last light . . . I would imagine that the world was held together by the courses they flew through the air." The momentum created by the piling of image upon image, of figure upon figure, is so powerful that when one reaches the end of the book—I have experienced this with all of Sebald's books, and others have mentioned it as well—one feels an irresistible compulsion to turn it over and begin again.

Yet there is something unsettling about the spell that Sebald's books weave; and it is not only the disequilibrium that is constantly evoked by the differences between fact and fiction, art and life—a state in which Sebald's narrator continually finds himself and that Sebald seeks to induce in the reader as well. It is a deeper paradox. In the first chapter of *Vertigo*, Sebald traces the adventures of the young Stendhal (then known as Marie Henri Beyle) in Napoleon's army, and comments on the writer's own difficulty in recollecting them: "Even when the images supplied by memory are true to life one can place little confidence in them." Years later Beyle will discover that he had replaced his own mental image of Ivrea with that of an engraving of the town. "This being so," Sebald concludes, "Beyle's advice is not to purchase engravings of fine views and prospects seen on one's travels, since before very long they will displace our memories completely, indeed one might say they destroy them."

Art is the preserver of memory, but it is also the destroyer of memory: this is the final tug-of-war in Sebald's work and the most fundamental one. As he searches for patterns in the constellation of grief that his books record, he runs the risk that the patterns themselves, by virtue of their very beauty, will extinguish the grief that they seek to contain. Sebald's peculiar alchemy of aestheticism and sorrow unwittingly underscores its own insubstantiality. Even as he investigates the roots of memory, Sebald, like the weavers whom he finds so emblematic, continually unravels his own creations.

II

For English readers, Sebald's books have an extra layer of circularity, because they appeared in translation out of order. *Vertigo*, his first prose book, was published in the United States after *The Emigrants* and *The Rings of Saturn*, and *Austerlitz* followed in 2001. Sebald's first literary work to be published in German, *After Nature*, was his last to appear in English. This displacement is actually a boon to English readers, because *After Nature* benefits immensely from being read after Sebald's other work. It is a panorama of many of his great themes, but they appear in embryonic form.

Like Sebald's other books, *After Nature* confounds genre: it has been called a prose poem, but while the language in places has the feel of prose, technically it is free verse. Each of the three sections has its own title and can be read as a distinct poem, but Sebald seems to have thought of them as a single entity. (In German the book is subtitled *Ein Elementargedicht*, "an elemental poem.") The volume's title refers to the practice of creating a work of art from a living subject (the poem mentions painting "after nature"), and the subject who is patiently submitting is Sebald himself: each of the three characters presented is a self-portrait of the writer. The first section is a biographical meditation on Matthias Grünewald, the sixteenth-century painter known for altarpieces that depict the crucifixion and other torments of the flesh and the soul with harrowing fidelity. (Max Ferber, the painter of *The Emigrants*, seems to speak for Sebald when he says that "the extreme vision of that strange man, which was lodged in every detail, distorted every limb, and infected the colors like an illness, was one I had always felt in tune with.") The second section follows eighteenth-century explorer Georg Wilhelm Steller (who shares Sebald's initials) on an Arctic journey led by Vitus Bering. And in the third Sebald investigates his own family history and early memories, much of which will prove fertile ground for the later works as well.

The suggestion of self-portraiture is evident from the opening lines of *After Nature*, which depict a person closing one of Grünewald's altar panels. As the panel folds in upon itself, the face of St. George becomes visible on the outside, "about to step over the frame's / threshold." George's "silver / feminine features" are those of Grünewald himself, whose face "emerges again and again / in his work." We are reminded of Sebald's own face and voice appearing over and over in his characters; and it heightens the analogy that the shape of the closed altar panel is reminiscent of a book, with the face of St. George—that is, of Grünewald—in the spot where the author's name should be.

Grünewald's face, Sebald continues, displays "always the same / gentleness, the same burden of grief, / the same irregularity of the eyes, veiled / and sliding sideways down into loneliness." Holbein the Younger, too, has depicted him in a painting of a female saint:

> These were strangely disguised
> instances of resemblance, wrote Fraenger
> whose books were burned by the fascists.
> Indeed it seemed as though in such works of art
> men had revered each other like brothers, and
> often made monuments in each other's
> image where their paths had crossed.

One could hardly ask for a better description of Sebald's own enterprise. Starting with this book, he would practice a somber cartography, mapping out in his own works of art the crossing paths, real or imagined, of Stendhal, Kafka, Nabokov, and the countless others whose suffering is stenciled on his work: "the marks of pain," as he put it in *Austerlitz*, "which . . . trace countless fine lines through history."

As the glancing reference above to "the fascists" shows, even when the events of World War II are not front and center in Sebald's book, they never recede far into the background. "We know there is a long tradition / of persecuting the Jews," the poem declares a bit later in this section and goes on to describe the torments suffered by the Jews of Frankfurt in the Middle Ages: a fiery massacre, the wearing of yellow rings, their confinement to a ghetto in which they were locked each night, and "on Sundays at four in the / afternoon." Grünewald would have witnessed this persecution, Sebald continues, because his future wife was reared in the ghetto, though she later converted to Christianity. But the persecution of the Jews is just a tile in the mosaic of human suffering, a mosaic that in this poem includes Grünewald's personal torments—his marriage was unhappy, possibly because "he had more of an eye for men"—as well as those of the patients in the hospital at Isenheim, the site of Grünewald's masterpiece, whose horrible disfigurements may have inspired some of the artist's work; and the massacre of five thousand peasants in the battle of Frankenhausen in 1525, which Grünewald learns of after meeting two painters who are brothers, Barthel and (yes) Sebald Beham. In Sebald's account Grünewald refused to leave his house after hearing of this, but

> he could hear the gouging out
> of eyes that long continued
> between Lake Constance and
> the Thuringian Forest.

For weeks at a time he wore
a dark bandage over his face.

But the dominant event is the solar eclipse of 1502, a "catastrophic incursion of darkness":

on the first of October the moon's shadow
slid over Eastern Europe from Mecklenburg
over Bohemia and the Lausitz to southern Poland,
and Grünewald, who repeatedly was in touch
with the Aschaffenburg Court Astrologer Johann
     Indagine,
will have travelled to see this event of the century,
awaited with great terror, the eclipse of the sun,
so will have become a witness to
the secret sickening away of the world,
in which a phantasmal encroachment of dusk
in the midst of daytime like a fainting fit
poured through the vault of the sky,
while over the banks of mist and the cold
heavy blues of the clouds
a fiery red arose, and colors
such as his eyes had not known
radiantly wandered about, never again to be
driven out of the painter's memory.
These colors unfold as the reverse of
the spectrum in a different consistency
of the air, whose deoxygenated void
in the gasping breath of the figures
on the central Isenheim panel is enough
to portend our death by asphyxiation; after which

comes the mountain landscape of weeping
in which Grünewald with a pathetic gaze
into the future has prefigured
a planet utterly strange, chalk-colored
behind the blackish-blue river.

Despite what the medievals may have thought, it is impossible now to see an eclipse as "catastrophic": the event simply does not merit the implication of horror. Sebald understands the eclipse, however, not as a single dreadful incident, but as part of a plumb line that descends through history, linking all the horrors that would take place in the same physical location, up to and including the Holocaust.

Later in the poem, similarly, Sebald discusses Altdorfer's painting of Lot and his daughters fleeing Sodom, in reference to the sight of Nuremberg in flames under the Allied bombs, and the epigraph to this section, from Virgil's *Eclogues*, draws the reader back even further: "and now far-off smoke pearls from homestead rooftops / and from high mountains the greater shadows fall." Though the conflagrations are distant from one another in every way—temporally, geographically—they are aesthetically part of a greater universal pattern of fiery massacre, a pattern that circles around infinitely, changed slightly upon each recurrence but not fundamentally altered. In later works Sebald has accomplished this kind of pattern tracing more effectively—here the layers can feel a bit slapped together—but the fundamental idea is the same: that when great suffering takes place somewhere, generation after generation, the sorrows are trodden in the soil.

But there is a crucial difference between the self-portrait and the artist: by witnessing one of the horrors that took place in this locale (the eclipse), Grünewald becomes a witness to them all. Sebald, on the other hand, witnessed none of World War II; and he feels this gap in his experience as painfully as most people feel the experience of trauma.

> I grew up,
> despite the dreadful course
> of events elsewhere, on the northern
> edge of the Alps, so it seems
> to me now, without any
> idea of destruction,

he writes in the poem's final, autobiographical section. Born in the penultimate year of the war in a remote German village, he was shielded from the destruction by virtue of his youth; but still as a child he imagined within him "a silent catastrophe that occurs / almost unperceived / . . . this / I have never got over."

Like Jacques Austerlitz and Max Ferber, Sebald sees himself as a child brought up unaware of his own identity, a Kaspar Hauser–like figure. The poem never fully reveals the source of the "silent catastrophe," the absent memory, but each part of this last autobiographical section sifts through a different time period in Sebald's life in search of clues. "For it is hard to discover / the winged vertebrates of prehistory / embedded in tablets of slate," the section begins, as if continuing a conversation, which in a way it is.

> But if I see before me
> the nervature of past life
> in one image, I always think
> that this has something to do
> with truth.

"How far, in any case, must one go back / to find the beginning?" Sebald asks. And the "beginning" for which he searches is that of his own prehistory. After passing over the day his grandparents were married and a few other potential "beginnings," he settles on the day before his father left to serve in Dresden, "of whose beauty his memory, as he / remarks when I question him, / retains no trace." The next night Nuremberg was attacked, and his mother, on her way back to the Allgäu, was stuck at a friend's house in the town of Windsheim, where she discovered that she was pregnant. The narrator's life, then, is indelibly intertwined with the last days of the war. And yet he can retain no memory of it; he was too young.

"I nearly went out of my mind," Sebald says of his reaction to seeing Altdorfer's painting in the Kunsthistorisches Museum in Vienna. Austerlitz will use exactly the same words to describe revisiting sites in Prague that he had not seen since childhood. Mourning the loss of a memory that he never had, Sebald turns to Altdorfer as a surrogate. When memory is lacking, art will suffice; but art is a shorthand, not a substitute. Sebald aestheticizes history, but he never mistakes history for art.

III

After Nature, the first of Sebald's literary works, inaugurates the search for "the nervature of past life" that would form the subtext of all his books. The character obsessively driven by a quest for knowledge—a quest rooted in his or her personal life—is a constantly recurring figure. Janine, a French professor in *The Rings of Saturn*, studies Flaubert's novels with "an intense personal interest" that is never explained. Jacques Austerlitz, a retired art history professor, has spent much of his life working on an investigation into the "family likeness" between various monuments of Europe, a topic that he feels compelled to pursue by an "impulse which he himself . . . did not really understand." Sebald's narrator can also be included in this category: though we encounter him at various points along his wanderings through Europe and America, we are never told why he makes his journeys.

But Sebald did write a book in which he explained what it was that possessed him so; and in doing so he ignited a controversy in Germany that one critic compared to the storm about Daniel Jonah Goldhagen's *Hitler's Willing Executioners.* Invited in 1997 to give a series of lectures at the University of Zurich, Sebald boldly put forth the thesis that postwar German literature had failed to represent adequately the devastating effects of the Allied bombing campaign for the German nation. The lectures were extensively covered in the Swiss and German media, and Sebald published them in book form in 1999 under the title *Luftkrieg und Literatur.*

The scale of the destruction caused by the bombings, Sebald argues, is difficult "to even halfway comprehend," but they "appear to have left hardly a trace of pain in the collective consciousness."* Not only did few German novelists concern themselves with the air war against Germany, Sebald says, but there exist almost no testimonies of the war written by Germans; the majority of the information about the destruction comes from foreign journalists reporting from the bombed-out nation. *Trummerliteratur,* the "rubble literature" movement

---

* Ruth Franklin's essay was written before Luftkrieg und Literatur was published in English in 2003 as *On the Natural History of Destruction.* The quoted passages are Franklin's translations and differ slightly from the published version, translated by Anthea Bell.

that emerged in the years immediately following World War II, is most notable for what Sebald calls its "collective amnesia." Even now that historians have begun to document the destruction of the German cities, "the images of this harrowing chapter of our history have not truly crossed the threshold of the national consciousness." Sebald describes a "tacit but universally valid agreement" among writers not to record the "true state of material and moral annihilation" in which the nation found itself—in other words, a conspiracy in German culture, the effects of which have lasted to this day.

What is needed to counteract this tendency, Sebald argues, is a "natural history of the destruction." He is generous with statistics: 1 million tons of bombs dropped, 131 cities hit, 600,000 civilians dead, 3.5 million homes destroyed, 7.5 million Germans left homeless. He cites Hans Erich Nossack on the streams of refugees that "noiselessly and incessantly flooded everything," bringing the chaos of the urban bombing into the quiet villages of the countryside. He devotes pages to the sudden flourishing of the parasites that feed off corpses: the rats, "bold and fat," that "cavorted in the streets"; the flies, "huge, iridescent green, as had never been seen before." And he remarks mordantly that "the striking paucity of observations and commentary on this matter can be explained by an unspoken taboo that is more understandable when one considers that the Germans, who had taken upon themselves the cleansing and hygienization of all of Europe, must have had to shield themselves from the mounting fear that they themselves were in fact the 'rat nation' [*Rattenvolk*]."

Though he is generally sympathetic to the German civilians who suffered so greatly, Sebald has harsh words for the way they closed their eyes to the destruction around them. Alfred

Döblin remarked that people "walk around as if nothing had happened and . . . the city had always looked like this." The Swedish journalist Stig Dagerman, reporting from Hamburg, recalled traveling on a train that passed through the "moon-scape" of that city; though the train was full, not a single person looked out the window. "And because he looked out the window," Sebald writes, "people recognized him as a foreigner." Nossack reported seeing a woman cleaning the windows of a house that "stands alone, undamaged, in the middle of the wasteland of ruins." Sebald finds something ghastly in this: we are unsurprised when the inhabitants of an insect colony do not weep over the destruction of a construction nearby, but "from humankind one expects a certain amount of empathy."

This is really beside the point, though, because the question concerns the responsibility of writers to respond to incidents in their culture, not the responsibility of the average citizen to open his eyes when confronted with the ugliness of humanity. (The German "amnesia" about the Allied bombing would hardly have been the Germans' first cognitive failure in those terrible years.) Sebald is correct about the profound absence of the bombing campaign in postwar German literature, but it is not as if German writers had chosen to ignore the war. They overwhelmingly concerned themselves with the war—I am thinking of Günter Grass, Heinrich Böll, Wolfgang Koeppen, Thomas Mann, Ingeborg Bachmann, Max Frisch, Siegfried Lenz, Gert Hofmann—but not with the *Luftkrieg* aspect of it. Indeed, in postwar German writing one finds almost an obsession with Nazism: its beginnings, its rise to power, its lingerings in German society long after the war, and not least its crimes. Based on the literary evidence, National Socialism may have been as earth-shaking for German society as the million tons of bombs that fell on German soil. If German writers did not begin to write about the destruction of their cities until the 1990s, this may be because it was simply not as important to them; and that is to their credit, a sign of historical conscience. It is hardly a moral delinquence to worry more about what you have done to others than about what others have done to you.

One could also ask, as many German critics did, whether it actually is the responsibility of literature to register the impact of contemporary events. And there were other criticisms of Sebald's argument as well. Kurt Oesterle, writing in the *Süddeutsche Zeitung*, pointed out that Sebald may have overestimated the eyewitness reports that make up so much of the basis for his arguments, reports that "shock before they explain." And Dieter Forte published a long and very personal article in *Der Spiegel* in which he argued that "there exists horror that is beyond language" and cited the Polish writer Andrzej Szczypiorski's comment that after he was released from a concentration camp he needed to "switch off his head" so that his body would survive. "Sebald prefers the indirect method, the clear reports, the clarity of calm observation; he remains distant from the actual horror, as if he were on the trail of one of his collages," Forte wrote. "He overlooks my generation, the generation of the children in the big cities, who can remember, when they are able, when they can find words for it—and for that one must wait an entire lifetime."

But these criticisms all overlook the aspect of Sebald's book that, for a non-German reader, is the most obvious, and the most shocking: the utterly ahistorical way in which Sebald discusses the bombing campaign, without giving even a hint of moral or political context. One could argue that everyone knew the context already and so it does not need to be reiterated. But in fact Sebald was misinterpreted by some as implicitly arguing that the sufferings of the Germans could be seen as compensatory for the crimes of the Nazis, as the letters from readers that he discusses in the third chapter of the book reveal. He tries to correct this, quoting from such letters and giving his responses, and ending with the comment that "the majority of Germans today know—at least so one hopes—that we directly provoked the destruction of the cities in which we lived." But in the first two chapters of his book—that is, the portion delivered as lectures—Sebald mentions the Holocaust only obliquely, and no other form of German aggression during World War II at all.

I do not mean in any way to suggest that Sebald was insensitive to the victims of the Holocaust. His literary work, especially *The Emigrants* and *Austerlitz*, shows him to be unique among German writers in his understanding of the catastrophe that befell the European Jews. Indeed, only a writer with Sebald's moral standing with regard to the Holocaust could have dared write such a book as this one. And yet parts of *Luftkrieg und Literatur* are weirdly lacking in this sensitivity. One hesitates to accuse Sebald of something so crass as "moral equivalency," but the suspicion of such a confusion cannot be avoided. On the very first page of the book Sebald calls the Allied bombings of Germany during the war "an act of extermination [*Vernichtungsaktion*] unique in history up to that point." Later he refers to the "incineration" [*Einascherung*] of the city of Hamburg. He knows as well as anyone what those words imply.

In Sebald's defense, one could argue that the Holocaust is simply not his subject here, that he is writing about an entirely different aspect of the war, and that to do justice to the Holocaust as well would have required an entirely different book.

But the book makes it hard to sustain such a defense. For *Luftkrieg und Literatur* goes even further. Most remarkable is the passage in which Sebald discusses the important role of music in Germany, even at the time of the bombings. He quotes an English journalist who said that "in the midst of such shambles only the Germans could produce a magnificent full orchestra and a crowded house of music lovers," and he rightly takes umbrage with this "double-edged" remark. And then he continues:

> Who would deny the audiences, who were listening then with glistening eyes to the music rising throughout the nation once again, the right to be moved by feelings of gratitude for their rescue? And the question must also be permitted as to whether their breasts did not swell with the perverse pride that no one in the history of mankind on earth had been so played upon and had withstood so much as the Germans.

"The history of mankind on earth"? This grandiose and categorical suggestion would be incredible even if it came from a mediocre German writer eager to come to terms with the past (say, Bernhard Schlink); but it is even more incredible coming from Sebald.

And yet in a way it is not so incredible. For Sebald's work has always presented suffering without its cause, as merely a part of the great pattern of pain that defines the human condition. We see this in the unique brand of melancholy that afflicts his characters, a melancholy that always seems to exist outside their comprehension. ("What was it that so darkened our world?" laments one character in *Austerlitz* on her deathbed.) Sebald's narrator, too, often makes remarks that summon the very depths of grief and then asserts that he "has no idea" why a particular image or anecdote affects him so. For all the empathy that Sebald seems to feel for the people in his books, this willful lack of understanding, this pretense to historical ignorance, is evidence of the "distance from actual horror" that Forte detects in his work. In order to trace the pattern of human suffering, one must have a certain disengagement from it—but at such a height things can begin to blur. And so Jews, Germans, and countless others are all equal elements of the design, equal parts of the mosaic.

Sebald's patterning amounts to an aestheticizing of catastrophe, and thus it annihilates causality. We appreciate the beauty of the image that the writer discerns, but it adds nothing to our understanding of why things happened as they did. And this is the great problem with a "natural history" of the bombings. The air war over Hitler's Germany was not a natural disaster, like the eclipse of 1502. It was not random in its causes or its effects; and so, morally speaking, it was worse than a natural disaster. The bombings may have the physical impact of an earthquake, but they cannot be understood in the same way, because to do so is to ignore the fact that this catastrophe was man-made, a human action, and thus more complicated and more terrible than another inevitable repetition of nature's rich but meaningless pattern of disaster. We must grieve for the terrible loss of innocent life that occurred in every arena in which World War II was fought, but we must also recognize that Hitler's aggression needed to be stopped.

In light of Sebald's views regarding art and memory, his arguments about the absence of German literature on the

Luftkrieg read a bit ironically. For this time the impairment is not a gap in memory, it is a gap in literature. But as we have seen, Sebald looks to art to fill gaps in memory, and the air war is his own biggest gap.

> I grew up with the feeling that something had been withheld from me—at home, in school, and also by the German writers whose books I read in the hope of being able to find out more about the enormity in the background of my own life.
>
> I spent my childhood and youth in a region on the northern edge of the Alps that was largely protected from the immediate effects of the so-called hostilities. At the end of the war I was just one year old and thus can hardly have retained impressions based on real experiences from that time of destruction. But even today, when I see photographs or documentaries of the war, I feel as if I stemmed from it, so to speak, and as if a shadow of these horrors, which I did not experience at all, had been cast over me from which I would never escape.

I sympathize deeply with Sebald's desire to resurrect a memory he never experienced. I have a similar desire to "remember" the Holocaust, which casts a shadow (to borrow his phrase) over my own life and that of my family. But gaps in memory are experience that is forever lost; and art cannot take its place. At the end of *The Emigrants*, the narrator visits an exhibition of photographs from the Lodz ghetto, and among them he sees a photograph of three women around the age of twenty behind a loom.

> The light falls on them from the window in the back-
> ground, so I cannot make out their eyes clearly, but I
> sense that all three of them are looking across at me,
> since I am standing on the very spot where Genewein the
> accountant stood with his camera. The young woman in
> the middle is blonde and has the air of a bride about
> her. . . . I wonder what the three women's names were—
> Roza, Luisa and Lea, or Nona, Decuma and Morta, the
> daughters of night, with spindle, scissors and thread.

I am strangely moved by this passage each time I read it,
because the young woman in the photograph could have been
my own grandmother, who was blonde and whose family owned
a textile factory in Lodz. I imagine her behind the loom, spin-
ning out my own fate: to pace the same ground over and over,
looking for the source of the shadow that still darkens my world.
Yet such a connection is dangerous, because it illustrates the illu-
sory workings of art against memory. My grandmother is not a
quasi-mythological figure peering out from behind a loom; she
is a real person whose experiences during the Holocaust cannot
be subsumed in the cycle of life's sorrows. I do not know what
she looked like as a young woman, but my imagining her behind
Sebald's loom, like Sebald's invocation of Altdorfer or Virgil to
describe Nuremberg, merely substitutes an artistic image for a
blank space. The blankness, however, is closer to the truth.

When it seeks to do the work of memory, art may be a
source of illusion. And Sebald may have had his own doubts
about his endeavor. As he wrote in *The Rings of Saturn*:

> That weavers in particular, together with scholars and
> writers with whom they had much in common,

tended to suffer from melancholy and all the evils associated with it, is understandable given the nature of their work, which forced them to sit bent over, day after day, straining to keep their eye on the complex patterns they created. It is difficult to imagine the depths of despair into which those can be driven who, even after the end of the working day, are engrossed in their intricate designs and who are pursued, into their dreams, by the feeling that they have got hold of the wrong thread.

I do not know whether Sebald despaired over his own complex patterns; but he recognized himself that the patterning and layering in his books closely resembles the Penelope-like embroidering and unraveling of the weavers who reappear throughout his pages. His material is memory, not thread, but the result is the same: a work of art that vanishes almost as soon as it appears, undone by the opposing forces that it seeks to mesh. And so Sebald's struggle against oblivion ends ironically in evanescence. The art that he created is of near miraculous beauty, but it is as fragile, and as ephemeral, as a pearl of smoke.

Conspiracy of Silence

by Charles Simic

I first read W. G. Sebald's *The Emigrants* when it came out in English in 1996 and remember feeling that I had not read anything so captivating in a long time. The book is difficult to classify. Told in the first person by the author, it reads at times like a memoir, at others like a novel or a work of nonfiction about the lives of four emigrants. They come from Lithuania and Germany and end up in England and the United States. The book includes, and this is another peculiarity of his, blurry, black-and-white photographs with no captions and not-always-clear connections to people and places being talked about in its pages. As for the author, one knew next to nothing about him except what one deduced from autobiographical details in the book, most importantly that he was a German living in England. *The Emigrants* was widely praised and called a masterpiece by many eminent writers and critics. The reviewers noted the author's elegiac tone, his grasp of history, his extraordinary powers of observation, and the clarity of his writing. While stressing his originality, critics mentioned Kafka, Borges, Proust, Nabokov, Calvino, Primo Levi, Thomas Bernhard, and a few others as Sebald's likely influences. There were some complaints about the unrelenting pessimism of his

Originally appeared in *The New York Review of Books*, February 27, 2003. Reprinted with permission from *The New York Review of Books*. Copyright © 2003 NYREV, Inc.

account of thwarted lives and the occasional monotony of his meandering prose, but even those who had reservations acknowledged the power of his work.

The narrator of *The Emigrants* is a loner and so are the rest of the characters. The countless victims of last century's wars, revolutions, and mass terror are what interests Sebald. One may say that he sought a narrative style that would convey the state of mind of those set adrift by forces beyond their understanding and control. Unlike men and women who have never known exile, whose biography is shaped by and large by social class and environment, to be a refugee is to have sheer chance govern one's fate, which in the end guarantees a life so absurd in most cases that it defeats anyone's powers of comprehension. Sebald served as a kind of oral historian and unconventional biographer of such people, reconstructing their lives out of bits and pieces he was told by them and out of additional research he did himself into their backgrounds. If his book is melancholy, it is because the task he gives himself is all but hopeless.

Another oddity of Sebald's prose, which either delights or exasperates his readers, is his digressions. He never hesitates to interject some interesting anecdote or bit of factual information arrived at by some not-always-apparent process of association. He does this without forewarning, transition, or even paragraph break. Clearly, he intends the reader to draw together the various threads in the book, the way one would do with images and metaphors in a poem, and make something of them. Here is an example from *The Rings of Saturn* (1998), which tells of an event from the 1860 British and French punitive military expedition into China and anticipates some of his concerns in *On the Natural History of Destruction*:

In early October the allied troops, themselves now uncertain how to proceed, happened apparently by chance on the magic garden of Yuan Ming Yuan near Peking, with its countless palaces, pavilions, covered walks, fantastic arbours, temples and towers. On the slopes of man-made mountains, between banks and spinneys, deer with fabulous antlers grazed, and the whole incomprehensible glory of Nature and of the wonders placed in it by the hand of man was reflected in dark, unruffled waters. The destruction that was wrought in these legendary landscaped gardens over the next few days, which made a mockery of military discipline or indeed of all reason, can only be understood as resulting from anger at the continued delay in achieving a resolution. Yet the true reason why Yuan Ming Yuan was laid waste may well have been that this earthly paradise—which immediately annihilated any notion of the Chinese as an inferior and uncivilized race—was an irresistible provocation in the eyes of soldiers who, a world away from their homeland, knew nothing but the rule of force, privation, and the abnegation of their own desires. Although the accounts of what happened in those October days are not very reliable, the sheer fact that booty was later auctioned off in the British camp suggests that much of the removable ornaments and the jewellery left behind by the fleeing court, everything made of jade or gold, silver or silk, fell into the hands of the looters. . . . The temples, palaces and hermitages, mostly built of cedarwood, went up in flames one after another with unbelievable speed, according to Charles George Gordon, a thirty-year-old captain in the Royal Engineers, the fire spreading through the green shrubs and woods, crackling and leaping. Apart from a few stone bridges and marble pagodas, all was destroyed. For a long time, swathes of smoke drifted over the entire area, and a great cloud of ash that obscured the sun was borne to Peking by the west wind, where after a time it settled on the heads and homes of those who, it was surmised, had been visited by the power of divine retribution.

The secret of Sebald's appeal is that he saw himself in what now seems almost an old-fashioned way as a voice of conscience, someone who remembers injustice, who speaks for those who can no longer speak. There was nothing programmatic about that. He wrote as if nothing else was worth a serious person's attention. Like anyone of us who takes time to read history, both ancient and modern, he was dismayed. No explanations along the lines of "war is hell," "human beings everywhere are like that," and so forth could make him forget for a moment the cruelties committed against the innocent. He'd agree with the Dowager Empress of China, who said before she died that she finally understood that history consists of nothing but misfortune, so that in all our days on earth we never know one single moment that is genuinely free of fear. What is strange—and it's no doubt owing to the marvelous translation of Michael Hulse, who worked closely with Sebald—is that the effect of his tales of horror is lyrical.

Vertigo, the very first prose book he wrote, when he was forty-six years old, was published in Germany in 1990 and not translated into English until 1999. It is a story of a journey across Europe in the footsteps of Stendhal, Casanova, and Kafka which ends in the narrator's native Bavarian village. *Austerlitz*, which followed in 2001 in a translation by Anthea Bell, is his one true novel. It is a story of a small child brought to England in one of the children transports from Germany in the summer of 1939 and his subsequent effort to find out about the death of his Jewish parents and his origins in Prague. Sebald said that behind the hero of the book hide two or three, or perhaps three and a half, real persons. Some of the narrative feels contrived with realistic description alternating with segments that could have come out of magic-realist fiction, and yet the book contains some of his best and his most moving writing.

I recall him saying in an interview that there are questions a historian is not permitted to ask, because they are metaphysical. The truth for him always lies elsewhere, somewhere yet undiscovered in myriad overlooked details of some individual existence. "I think how little we can hold in mind," he writes after a visit to a Belgian prison used by the Nazis, "how everything is constantly lapsing into oblivion with every extinguished life, how the world is, as it were, draining itself, in that the history of countless places and objects which themselves have no power of memory is never heard, never described or passed on."

There's a spooky scene in *Austerlitz* in which the hero, walking the empty streets of Terezin in Czechoslovakia where his mother had died in a camp, comes upon a closed antique store window cluttered with various objects that in all probability belonged to the inmates. There they were, these ornaments, utensils, and mementos that had outlived their former owners together with his own faint shadow image barely perceptible among them. All that remained was a Japanese fan, a globe-shaped paperweight, and a miniature barrel organ that brought home the reality of some vanished life and the magnitude of what happened.

Sebald's posthumous book, *On the Natural History of Destruction*, again has four parts and reads this time like a straightforward collection of nonfiction pieces. The subject of the first is the destruction of German cities by Allied bombing. The other three, which were not included in the original German edition, deal with the postwar German novelist Alfred Andersch; the Austrian-Belgian writer Jean Améry, who survived Auschwitz; and the painter Peter Weiss. The chapters on the air war were based on lectures he delivered in the autumn of 1997 in Zurich. His thesis, which provoked considerable controversy when the lectures were published in newspapers in Germany, is that the destruction of all the larger German cities and many smaller ones by the Allied air raids was never adequately discussed in literature after the war. There was a conspiracy of silence about it as there was about many other things that occurred during the Nazi years.

This is not exactly a new discovery. Hans Magnus Enzensberger essentially made the same point in an essay called "Europe in Ruins" that he wrote in 1990. In contrast to Heinrich Böll, Primo Levi, Hans Werner Richter, Louis-Ferdinand Céline, Curzio Malaparte, and a number of foreign journalists, practically all German storytellers avoided the subject. So why did Sebald bring it up again?

Some accused him of being motivated by a need to have the Germans perceived as victims and thus minimize the suffering of others by creating a moral equivalence. This is completely unfair to him. Sebald knew that Germans provoked the annihilation of their cities and that they would have done the same and worse to others had they been able to. His detractors seem to believe that there is a moral scale by which the suffering of the innocent among different ethnic groups can be calculated, with the most deserving at the top and those least deserving of pity at the bottom, and they are shocked that he lacked their faith. The issues he raises about the war against the civilians have no simple answers. They defy description.

> Today it is hard to form an even partly adequate idea of the extent of the devastation suffered by the cities of Germany in the last years of the Second World War, still harder to think about the horrors involved in that devastation. It is true that the strategic bombing surveys published by the Allies, together with the records of the Federal German Statistics Office and other official sources show that the Royal Air Force alone dropped a million tons of bomb on enemy territory; it is true that of the 131 towns and cities attacked, some only once and some repeatedly, many were almost entirely flattened, that about 600,000 German civilians fell victim to the air raids, and that three and a half million homes were destroyed, while at the end of the war seven and a half million people were left homeless, and there were 31.1 cubic meters of rubble for every person in Cologne and 42.8 cubic meters for every inhabitant of Dresden—but we do not grasp what it all actually meant.

In view of the number of civilian casualties in bombings of urban areas in the last century, there are reasons to think it may be safer to be a soldier at the front than a mother with children sitting in a cellar during an air raid. The figures for deaths in individual German cities are staggering, but they are equally horrendous elsewhere. Forty-three thousand died in the London Blitz; 100,000 in Tokyo in 1945, plus Hiroshima and Nagasaki where over 200,000 perished; and the list goes on. More recently there is Vietnam, where an estimated 365,000 civilians died, and finally Baghdad in the Gulf War for which the figures are kept secret. In Japan, not counting the atom bombs, over 300,000 civilians perished just in 1945. Of course, these rounded-off figures are at best educated guesses. Bombing history plays games with numbers to conceal the individuals' fates. The deaths of the innocent are an embarrassment. All religious and secular theories of "just war" from Saint Augustine to the United Nations Charter caution against their indiscriminate slaughter. The Geneva Convention warns the parties to the conflict again and again to distinguish between civilian populations and combatants, and between civilian objectives and military objectives.

Since civilians, by international agreement, are not supposed to be the object of attack, the numbers for what we today call euphemistically "collateral damage" tend to vary widely in retrospect depending on the political agenda of the writer. Even when they are plainly given, they sound as inconceivable as astronomical distances. A number like 100,000 conveys horror on an abstract level. A figure like 100,001, on the other hand, would be far more alarming in my view. That lone additional person would restore the reality to the thousands of other casualties. To thumb through a book of old news photos or watch documentary footage of an air raid in progress is a sobering experience. One of the most common sights of the last century is a row of burned and still smoldering buildings of which only the outside walls remain. Rubble lies in the streets. The sky is black except for dragons of flames and swirling smoke. We know that there are people buried under the rubble. I remember a photo of a small naked girl running toward a camera in a bombed village somewhere in Vietnam. After almost a hundred years of this sort of thing, it takes a staggering insensitivity not to acknowledge what a bombing raid on a populated area does and who its true victims are.

I myself remember the firebomb from my childhood in Yugoslavia. It carries sticks of explosive that burst into flames. The sticks scatter loosely like straws in a game of jackstraws, each one a fire starter. If the weather is dry and there is a bit of wind, such bombs can start a firestorm that can wrap an entire city in a blanket of fire. The glow of such fires, pilots report, is visible a hundred miles away, and even the smell of burning buildings and human beings ablaze like matches reaches the high-flying planes. I knew a boy who lost both arms attempting to dismantle such a bomb. In World War II, there was also the famous bomb cocktail in which different incendiaries were used to start fires on the roof, bigger bombs to penetrate all the way down to the cellar, and the heaviest ones to blow in windows and doors and make huge craters in the streets, so the fire engines could not reach the fires. Dante's and Jonathan Edwards's ghastly descriptions of hell pale in comparison to airmen's descriptions of what it was like to conduct and witness the effects of these raids.

It's not just the droning planes, the bloodred skies, and the deafening explosions that are frightening. Even more scary is the power of those who give themselves the right to decide whom to obliterate, whom to spare. It cannot be helped, is their excuse. If they are right, and I'm not convinced they are, that may be the most terrifying thing of all. No matter what history books have told us, bombing is a form of collective punishment premised on collective guilt. Prominent theoreticians of air power have never concealed that. In a war, they argue, there cannot be a differentiation made between military personnel and civilians. Especially when it comes to a nation like Germany, whose leaders ordered that millions of people be murdered and worked to death, and many of whose citizens carried out the orders, it is hard to feel sorry. The firestorms were universally regarded as a just punishment even if they didn't have much military and political logic, as is now fairly clear from the documentary evidence. I understand the emotion perfectly. I grew up hating Germans.

But—and this is the crux of the matter—can dropping bombs on densely populated residential areas really be justified? Can one hold the view that women and children of the enemy are not blameless and still pretend to have an ethical position? Are deaths of noncombatants truly of so little consequence? The answer—judging by the long, cruel history of last century's bombings—is yes. Killing innocents is thought to be a necessary evil. To that I'd say—and I speak from experience—that for those who are bombed it feels like destruction for its own sake. Since the bombs can hardly ever get at the leaders wining and dining in their well-protected underground shelters, the innocent will always have to pay for their crimes.

"How ought such a natural history of destruction to begin?" Sebald asks. He wants us to ponder what it means to have an entire city with all its buildings, trees, inhabitants, domestic pets, fixtures, and fittings destroyed. The remains of human beings are everywhere, flies swarm around them, the floors and steps of the cellar are thick with slippery finger-length maggots, rats and flies rule the city. The few eyewitness accounts are ghastly. In the midst of rubble, out of sheer panic, the population tries to carry on as if nothing has happened. There's a woman, for instance, washing a window of a building that stands in a desert of ruins. No wonder survivors found it difficult to talk about it. Sebald's parents would not. He grew up, he says, with the feeling that something was being kept from him at home, at school, and by the German writers he read hoping to glean more information about these events.

Silence about what happened to their cities was not just a German reaction. Twenty years after the bomb fell on Hiroshima most of the survivors could not speak of what happened that day. My mother, who lay next to me in the cellar during many an air raid on Belgrade, wouldn't talk about it either. In his books Sebald has always been interested in the way in which individual, collective, and cultural memory deal with experiences that lie on the border of what language can convey. Bombing is part of that, but there are other, even more terrible things human beings have had to cope with. In what is in my view the best essay in *On the Natural History of Destruction*, he quotes Jean Améry's description of being tortured by the Gestapo:

> In the bunker there hung from the vaulted ceiling a chain that above ran into a roll. At its bottom end it bore a heavy, broadly curved iron hook. I was led to the instrument. The hook gripped into the shackle that held my hands together behind my back. Then I was raised with the chain until I hung about a metre above the floor. In such a position, or rather, when

hanging this way, with your hands behind your back, for a short time you can hold at a half-oblique through muscular force. During these few minutes, when you are already expending your utmost strength, when sweat has already appeared on your forehead and lips, and you are breathing in gasps, you will not answer any questions. Accomplices? Addresses? Meeting places? You hardly hear it. All your life is gathered in a single, limited area of the body, the shoulder joints, and it does not react; for it exhausts itself completely in the expenditure of energy. But this cannot last long, even with people who have a strong physical constitution. As for me, I had to give up rather quickly. And now there was a cracking and splintering in my shoulders that my body has not forgotten to this hour. The balls sprang from their sockets. My own body weight caused luxation; I fell into a void and now hung by my dislocated arms which had been torn high from behind and were now twisted over my head. Torture, from Latin *torquere*, to twist. What visual instruction in etymology!

Sebald admires the Belgian resistance fighter's detachment and understatement which prohibits both pity and self-pity. Only at the very end of his account, in that one ironic phrase which concludes a "curiously objective passage," as Sebald says, is it clear that his composure has reached a breaking point. If someone wanted to convey truly what it was like, Améry went on to say, he would be forced to inflict pain and thereby become a torturer himself. The utter helplessness of human beings in such circumstances, deep pity, and solidarity with victims of injustice are the recurring themes for both of these men. Sebald quotes a diary entry of one Friedrich Reck who tells of a group of refugees from bombing trying to force their way into a train at a station in Upper Bavaria. As they do, a cardboard suitcase "falls on the platform, bursts open and spills its contents. Toys, a manicure case, singed underwear. And last of all the roasted corpse of a child, shrunk like a mummy, which its half-deranged mother has been carrying about with her."

It's all just too much, one says to oneself reading such a passage. What worries Sebald, as it should worry any thinking person, is our newfound capacity for total destruction. Is it ever morally justified to fight evil with evil? It continues to be a worry despite what our most passionate warmongers and strategists tell us almost daily about the so-called smart bombs and mini-nukes which will spare the innocent and target only the guilty. For instance, the Pentagon's current war plan for Iraq, according to CBS, calls for a launch of four hundred cruise missiles on the first day, which is more than were launched during the entire forty days of the Gulf War, with the same number to follow the next day and presumably the day after.

The battle plan is based on a concept developed at the National Defense University. It's called "Shock and Awe" and it focuses on the psychological destruction of the enemy's will to fight rather than the physical destruction of his military forces. "We want them to quit. We want them not to fight," says Harlan Ullman, one of the authors of the Shock and Awe concept which relies on large numbers of precision-guided weapons. "So that you have this simultaneous effect, rather like the nuclear weapons at Hiroshima, not taking days or weeks but in minutes," says Ullman. In the first Gulf War, 10 percent of the weapons were precision-guided. In this war, 80 percent will be precision-guided.

I have my doubts and I imagine Sebald would have them too. So much intellect, capital, and labor go into the planning of destruction, one can count on excuses being found in the future for some inadvertent slaughter. The ones who survive will again be faced with the same problem: how to speak of the unspeakable and make sense of the senseless.

Crossing Boundaries

by Arthur Lubow

As a child in a Bavarian village in the lean years after the Second World War, W. G. Sebald constructed his own playthings. "If you grow up not with toys bought in the shop but things that are found around the farmyard, you do a sort of bricolage," he told me. "Bits of string and bits of wood. Making all sorts of things, like webs across the legs of a chair. And then you sit there, like the spider." We were talking about the idiosyncratic way in which he composed his books. He said that the urge "to connect bits that don't seem to belong together" had fascinated him all his life.

I was visiting Sebald in Norwich, England, in August—a few weeks before the publication of what proved to be his last novel, *Austerlitz*—in order to write a profile for the *New York Times Magazine*. The September 11 attacks and the Afghanistan war intervened, so that the piece did not run until December, and then at reduced length in the daily newspaper. Three days after the article appeared, Sebald died in an accident. Once the first shock of the news had receded, I rethought our conversations, connecting the pieces differently in this stark new light. The jokes about attractive ways of dying, the descriptions of the book in progress, the vacillations

---

From "A Symposium on W. G. Sebald," *The Threepenny Review*, Spring 2002.

over postretirement plans—all took on unintended irony and unwelcome poignancy. But I was unsure whether these new associations were instructive or merely distracting.

Writing before Sebald's death, I hadn't felt the need to devote much space to the book he was working on. Now that the book would never be born, I wondered if my jottings on his remarks (like an architect's unbuilt doodle) possessed a new value. And what about his future? In two years he would have been able to step down with a full pension from his position teaching literature at the University of East Anglia. Because he wrote so eloquently about the sense of dislocation, I had asked if there was any place he had ever felt at home, and that line of talk had led to his musing about where he might spend his final years. Did those dreams, brutally foreclosed, become irrelevant or somehow more important?

Thinking about Sebald, I slipped into Sebaldian logic. The boundaries between the dead and the living, the planned and the accomplished, the remembered and the real, came to seem arbitrary. In one of our conversations, he had approvingly described the custom in traditional Corsican households of consulting the portraits of ancestors before making important decisions. "These borders between the dead and the living are not hermetically sealed," he said. "There is some form of travel or gray zone. If there is a feeling, especially among unhappy people, that there is such a thing as a living death, then it is possible that the *revers* is also true." That the book and the retirement would never occur didn't much change the valence of the material. Reading Sebald, you feel the excitement of exploring a strange new landscape. The bits I had gathered could serve as road markers—or, at least, travel posters—for the territory of his mind.

Sebald was "Proustian," people often said. Since his tone was elegiacal and his sentence structure was serpentine, that pigeonholing arose predictably. Furthermore, Sebald and Proust were alike in their creation of a unique format; one might aptly say of Sebald's books, as Walter Benjamin once wrote of Proust's, that "all great works of literature found a genre or dissolve one." That said, it strikes me that the differences between Sebald and Proust are more instructive than the similarities. When people call something Proustian, they are usually referring to Proust's fascination with involuntary memory, the way in which sensory associations conjure up the past. Yet the French writer elaborated just as extravagantly on the joys and tortures of anticipation. (The present moment is what disappointed him.) Sebald, temperamentally, preferred to keep his eyes averted from the future, which for him impended heavily with disaster. And he accumulated his recollections not in windfalls, but through diligent dredging and mining. Having been born in Germany in 1944 and raised in a society that willed itself into amnesia, he regarded remembering as a moral and political act. He described for me his first visit to Munich in 1947, as a three-year-old with his parents. While their village in the foothills of the Bavarian Alps escaped the war undamaged, Allied bombing devastated Munich. "You might have a few buildings standing intact and between them an avalanche of scree that had come down," he recalled. "And people didn't comment on it." He would not have thought to ask about the debris, and if he had, his parents would have evaded the question. "It seemed to me the natural condition of cities," he said, "houses between mountains of rubble." His father, an officer promoted up through the ranks, never discussed his wartime experiences. When I said offhandedly that by now his mother, in her late eighties, could probably no longer remember the

war years, he replied quickly, speaking of his mother's generation: "They could remember if they wanted to."

Scrutinizing documents—photographs, diaries, war
records—launched Sebald into a receptive state. (In *The Emigrants,* he wrote that looking at photographs, we feel "as if the
dead were coming back, or as if we were on the point of joining them.") He chose the objects of his attention intuitively.
Unlike a professional historian, who goes into a library with a
research plan, he foraged impulsively, then moved on. "I can't
afford to sit in the Munich War Archive for two years," he told
me. "So I have to rush in and sit there for a week or two and
collect things like someone who knows he has to leave before
too long. You gather things up like a person who leaves a burning house, which means very randomly." He accumulated
postcards from junk shops, maps from archives, passages from
memoirs. He tore photos from magazines or snapped them
himself with a little Canon. He used these images as a research
tool or an inspirational device, but he then chose to incorpo-
rate them into his books. "It's one way of making obvious that
you don't begin with a white page," he said. "You do have
sources, you do have materials. If you create something that
seems as if it proceeded seamlessly from your pen, then you
hide the material sources of your work."

Insidiously, the photographs also make the text appear to be
not fictional but real, despite the widespread knowledge that
even in the predigital age, photographs could be manipulated.
In *The Emigrants* a character remarks that a photograph published in the Nazi press that showed a book burning in
Würzburg in 1933 was fraudulent. Because the bonfire raged at
night, the cameras failed to record it; so a plume of smoke and
a nocturnal sky were added to a daytime shot of another gath-

ering. The narrator says that he was skeptical of this report until he unearthed the photograph himself and observed the obvious falsification. And at this point in the text, Sebald includes the image. "I had that picture," he explained. "I thought very consciously that this is a place to make a declaration. It couldn't be more explicit. It acts as a paradigm for the whole enterprise. The process of making a photographic image, which purports to be the real thing and isn't anything like, has transformed our self-perception, our perception of each other, our notion of what is beautiful, our notion of what will last and what won't." For Sebald, there could be no better touchstone for the importance and difficulty of getting to the truth than a doctored document of the Nazi destruction of the written word.

At the time of his death, Sebald was researching a book that would explore, among other subjects, his family history. "As they all came from the lower classes, there are often not even exact dates of birth or places of residence," he told me. "This uncertainty begins two generations back." His ancestors inhabited a forested region between Bavaria and Bohemia that had, from the time of the seventeenth century, been devoted to glassworks, and so Sebald could speculate with reasonable confidence about their working life. But even of that he was never quite certain. Like an archeologist reconstructing a pot from a couple of shards, he worked in a way that he characterized as "extremely tenuous and unreliable." In *The Rings of Saturn*, he compared writers to weavers: melancholics working complex patterns, always fearful that they have gotten hold of the wrong thread. One of the threads he was tracing in his next book concerned a commander of the Red Army in the short-lived Bavarian Socialist Republic.

Executed in Munich in 1919, on a spot that is now a Hermès store on posh Maximilianstrasse, this man had the same name as Sebald's mother's family. While Sebald had not established a family connection, what was at the least a coincidence had caught his attention.

At other stages of his research, a surfeit of unreliable documentation would cloud the picture further. For the same book, he was reading through twenty-three volumes of diaries (each consisting of two hundred pages, written in a minuscule hand, in ink made from elderberry fruit) that had been kept from 1905 into the 1950s by the grandfather of a friend of his, a Frenchwoman his age named Marie, who grew up in Picardy. This diarist grandfather, a miller, "was obviously the family scribe and the family rememberer, and yet he wasn't always accurate," Sebald said. "He took notes and he didn't always write them down at once, but in the evenings or on Sundays, because he was working." Relatives offered variant versions of the same events. "So there are all these different narratives, and they have equal rights and equal status," Sebald said. And in some places, of course, there are simply gaps. "You can say once or twice that the evidence is scarce, but you can't do that on every page—it becomes a bore. So you borrow things. You adulterate the truth as you try to write it. There isn't that pretense that you try to arrive at the literal truth. And the only consolation when you confess to this flaw is that you are seeking to arrive at the highest truth."

Marie's family in France had endured an intimately unhappy relationship with the Germans. Her grandfather's village was located near St. Quentin, right on the German defensive trench line in the last year of World War I. During World War II, her father joined the Resistance and was murdered by the Nazis. "He was shot at the age of twenty-two or twenty-three and had his eyes gouged out," Sebald said. Marie was born a few months later. Sebald showed me a photograph snapped by a Catholic priest of the austere stone building where the execution took place. "I think there is something there that you wouldn't get hold of without the photograph," he said. "Not necessarily to be put in the book, but for the working process. Certain things emerge from the images if you look at them long enough."

He showed me a topographical map from 1918 used by the German army command: "This gives you an idea of the density of the trench system, the irrationality of it . . . The completely insane collective effort that marks this event—I don't think I shall be able to understand it, but I want to marvel at it." Whenever he visited Munich, Sebald would spend half a day at the War Archive, calling up volumes that no one had touched in decades. He recalled the first time that the files that he had ordered arrived on a trolley. "You have a visual sense of how much something weighs," he said. "You try to pick this up, and you can barely lift it. It's as if the specific weight of the paper they used is higher than the paper we use. Or it's as if the dust has gotten in there and insinuated itself, so they have become like a rock. If you have any imagination, you can't help but wonder about it. These are questions a historian is not permitted to ask, because they are of a metaphysical nature. And if one thing interests me, it is metaphysics." He paused for a second. "I am not seeking an answer," he said. "I just want to say, 'This is very odd, indeed.'"

Much of modern life repelled Sebald. He told me that one of the chief reasons he departed Germany, first for French-speaking Switzerland, then for England, was that he "found it

agreeable not to hear current German spoken all around me."
His literary models wrote in nineteenth-century German—
Gottfried Keller, Adalbert Stifter, Heinrich von Kleist, Jean Paul
Richter. "The contemporary language is usually hideous, but
in German it's especially nauseating," he said. He asked me if I
knew the German word for "mobile phone." With a look of
horror, he told me: a *handi*.

He owned neither a fax machine nor a telephone answer-
ing machine. He was the only faculty member at the
University of East Anglia without a computer in his office: he
had declined the one allotted him, recommending that the
money be used instead for student aid. ("Was it?" I asked. He
shrugged. "Of course not.") Amused by human foibles, his
own very much included, he knew that there was something
comical about his reactionary posture. "I hold with the wire-
less and the motor-car," he proclaimed. "I don't especially
appreciate the blessings of technology." Passively but stub-
bornly, he fought off the tawdry intrusions of the modern
world. "There's always an argument that is hard to resist," he
observed. "So your daughter says, 'What if I get stranded in
the middle of Thetford Forest in my not very reliable car—
shouldn't I have a mobile phone?' The devil comes in with a
carte de visite. That is always the way."

The gigantism of modernity—the scale of the buildings, the
acceleration of pace, the profusion of choices—afflicted Sebald
with a kind of vertigo. Ill at ease with the time in which he lived,
he may have felt most comfortable in a place in which he was
foreign. "I don't feel at home here in any sense," he said of Norwich, where he lived for thirty years. Drawn repeatedly to the
stories of people whose accents, native landscapes, and histories
mirrored his own, he never failed, when he visited his mother

in the town in which he was raised, to be disgusted by "all the nasty people in the street" who were "as boxed in as they have always been." His favorite subject was the Germans who had been cast out of their boxes, often Jews who had been forced to flee Nazi Germany. He insisted, persuasively, that he was not interested in Judaism or in the Jewish people for their own sake. "I have an interest in them not for any philo-Semitic reasons," he told me, "but because they are part of a social history that was obliterated in Germany and I wanted to know what happened." He felt a rapport with displaced people in general, and in particular, with outcast writers. "I can read the memoirs of Chateaubriand about his childhood in Brittany and find it very moving," he told me. "I can feel a closeness to him that may be greater than the proximity I feel to the people I find around me." His desire to know just a few people and places probably stemmed from this profound sense of dislocation. He derided the promiscuity of contemporary travel. "That is what is so awful about our modern life—we never return," he said. "One year we go to India and the next year to Peru and the next to Greenland. Because now you can go everywhere. I would much rather have half a dozen places that meant something to me than to say, at the end of my life, 'I have been practically everywhere.' The first visit doesn't reveal very much at all."

When I asked if there was any place in which he had ever felt at home, he thought of one spot, which not coincidentally has a literary pedigree: the island of St. Pierre in the Lac de Bienne in Switzerland, famous as the refuge of Rousseau in 1765. "I felt at home, strangely, because it is a miniature world," he said. "One manor house, one farmhouse. A vineyard, a field of potatoes, a field of wheat, a cherry tree, an orchard. It has one of everything, so it is in a sense an ark. It is like when you draw a place when you are a child. I don't like large-scale things, not in architecture or evolutionary leaps. I think it's an aberration. This notion of something that is small and self-contained is for me both an aesthetic and moral ideal." Although St. Pierre was not a realistic retirement choice, Sebald thought he might spend his final years in a French-speaking region, probably Switzerland. "With someone like me, you always have two sides," he said. "'Oh, I'll just move to the most beastly part of northern France and live in rented accommodations in St. Quentin or Combray and see if I survive.' But naturally there is another part of me that thinks of moving near Neuchâtel in Switzerland. I know that drawing up a plan makes no sense, because plans are never followed. It will be a question of constellations."

Although he made his living within the academy, Sebald made his reputation by deviating from the academic path. His first nonconformist book, *After Nature*, was a prose poem that resembled a Cubist self-portrait. In it, he discusses the sixteenth-century painter Matthias Grünewald, who was from Würzburg, not far from Sebald's hometown, and a young botanist, Georg Wilhelm Steller, who not only hailed from southern Germany but also shared Sebald's initials. The book ends with what Sebald described to me as "this pseudobiographical part about growing up in southern German in the postwar years."

Again and again, Sebald returned to figures who were rooted in or somehow connected to southern Germany. Like many lesser writers, he was primarily interested in himself; what redeemed this solipsism was the extraordinary and capacious nature of that self. The form that he devised for his writing (which he called, with uncharacteristic inelegance, "prose fiction") was a rumination or meditation in which all of the characters shared the rueful, melancholic tone of the narrator.

In *Austerlitz*, he tried to cleave more closely to the structure of a traditional novel, propelling the narrative forward with the saga of a man's search for his parents, and you could feel the author's unconventional mind creaking against the walls of convention. The new book promised to return to the free-ranging, more musical structure of the earlier ones, as seemed natural for someone who deprecated the ability of the old-fashioned novel to function in modern times. "There is so often about the standard novel something terribly contrived, which somewhere along the line tends to falter," he said. "The business of having to have bits of dialogue to move the plot along is fine for an eighteenth- or nineteenth-century novel, but that becomes in our day a bit trying, where you always see the wheels of the novel grinding and going on. Very often you don't know who the narrator is, which I find unacceptable. The story comes through someone's mind. I feel I have the right to know who the person is and what his credentials are. This has been known in science for a long time. The field of vision changes according to the observer, so I think this has to be part of the equation." He cautioned that the narrator was of course not to be confused with an "authentic person." In other words, the narrator of Sebald's novels was not to be mistaken for Sebald himself.

Notwithstanding the disclaimer, the joy of reading Sebald is the pleasure of stepping into the quirky treasure-house of his mind. "I don't consider myself a writer," he said. "It's like someone who builds a model of the Eiffel Tower out of matchsticks. It's a devotional work. Obsessive." His books are like some eighteenth-century *Wunderkammer*, filled with marvelous specimens, organized eccentrically. Even without the inclusion of the blurry black-and-white photographs that became a trademark, they would feel like journals or notebooks. Sebald himself, when I asked why every character in his novels sounded like the narrator, said, "It's all relayed through this narrative figure. It's as he remembers, so it's in his cast." He credited the monologues of Thomas Bernhard, in which the layers of attribution can run four deep, as an influence. Like an old-fashioned newspaper reporter in the era before blind quotes, Sebald believed in naming sources. "Otherwise, there's either the 'she said with a disconsolate expression on her face' or 'as thoughts of regret passed through her mind,'" he complained. "How does he know? I find it hard to suspend my disbelief." He was a literary magistrate who admitted nothing but hearsay as evidence. Or, to put it more precisely, he thought that a statement can no longer be evaluated once it is prised from the mind which gives it utterance.

In person, Sebald was funnier than his lugubrious narrators. He was celebrated among those lucky enough to hear him as a witty raconteur. Of course, one knows not to confuse a narrator and his author; but as I was reminded when speaking with Sebald, that admonition is merely one corollary of the impossibility of knowing with assurance another person's mind. "Say you write fairly gloomy things," he told me. "They think they should sue you under the Trade Description Act if you tell a joke. Who's to say? What you reveal in a dark text may be closer to the real truth than the person who tells a joke at a party." Some of his own melancholia came to him as a personal legacy: both his father and grandfather spent the last years of their lives morbidly depressed. His father, who in Sebald's telling resembled a caricature of the pedantic, subservient, frugal German, didn't like to read books. "The only book I ever saw him read was one my younger sister gave him for Christmas, just at the beginning of the ecological movement, with a name like *The End of the Planet*," Sebald said. "And my father was bowled over by it. I saw him underlining every sentence of it—with a ruler, naturally—saying, '*Ja, ja*.'"

Sebald's talk often turned to death, which he regarded with the same dry, wry eye that he cast on life. When I asked him casually why he had changed publishers, expecting the usual tale of finances and contracts and agents, he instead explained that it had all begun with the mysterious suicide of his German publisher, who hopped the S-Bahn to the mountains outside Frankfurt, drank half a bottle of liquor, took off his jacket, and lay down to die in the snow. "When hypothermia sets in, it's apparently quite agreeable," Sebald said. "Like drowning," I said. To which Sebald replied, with a nod, "Drowning also is quite agreeable."

He dated his own fascination with the no longer living to the death of his maternal grandfather. At the time Max was twelve, and his gentle, soft-spoken grandfather had been his hiking companion and confidant. "My interest in the departed, which has been fairly constant, comes from that moment of losing someone you couldn't really afford to lose," he said. "I broke out in a skin disease right after his death, which lasted for years." Was that where his interest in death began? A few moments later, paging through a family photo album from 1933, he pointed to a photograph that his father took of a fellow soldier who had died in a motor accident. Lying on his back, his unseeing eyes staring upward, the dead young man is surrounded by flowers. Seeing this picture for the first time at the age of five, Max had "a hunch that this is where it all began—a great disaster that occurred, which I knew nothing about." So perhaps this image of a corpse is where it commenced, his fascination with both photographs and death. Then he turned to another photograph, a finely detailed print of two women in mid-calf-length dresses and a man in leder-hosen and loden jacket standing in a neatly tended flower garden in front of a tile-roofed Bavarian-style chalet. These are Sebald's parents and a woman whose husband has snapped the picture. The photograph was taken in August 1943 in a park near Bamberg. The women are chic, cheerful, and prosperous looking. There are no swastika banners, no signs of wartime privation, and certainly no Jews in striped uniforms. You would not guess that less than thirty miles away is Nuremberg, seat of the Nazi Party rallies, a medieval city fated to be laid waste by Allied bombers the next year. Or that the man, Sebald's father, is home on an army furlough. But the Nazi regime flickers in this picture as a ghost image: everything here has been state approved, including the name Winfried Georg, which would be given to the child conceived on this furlough, a boy who would rather be called Max.

According equal status to the living and the dead—after all, they jostled side by side for space in his mind—Sebald would perhaps view his own passing with equanimity. He is spared the labor of writing the next book. For the rest of us, not having that book to look forward to is a blow, a subtracted hope. I am reminded of Sebald's account of an experiment that intrigued him. "They put a rat in a cylinder that is full of water and the rat swims around for about a minute until it sees that it can't get out and then it dies of cardiac arrest," he told me. A second rat is placed in a similar cylinder, except that this cylinder has a ladder, which enables the rat to climb out. "Then, if you put this rat in another cylinder and don't offer it a ladder, it will keep swimming until it dies of exhaustion," he explained. "You're given something—a holiday to Tenerife or you meet a nice person—and so you carry on, even though it's quite hopeless. That may tell you everything you need to know." He chuckled. Disconsolately, merrily, companionably, bitterly, resignedly, darkly, theatrically, dourly, inconsolably? One is in no position to say.

CONTRIBUTORS

CAROLE ANGIER was educated at McGill, Oxford, and Cambridge universities. She is the author of *Jean Rhys: Life and Work* and *The Double Bond: Primo Levi: A Biography*. In 2002 she was elected fellow of the Royal Society of Literature. She is the founder and teacher of The Practice of Biography at Warwick University and now teaches modern biography at Birkbeck College, University of London. She is currently working on *Writing Biography, Autobiography and Memoir*.

JOSEPH CUOMO has recently completed his first novel. He is also the director of Queens College Evening Readings, which he founded in 1976.

RUTH FRANKLIN has been an editor at *The New Republic* since 1999. Her criticism also appears in *The New Yorker*, *The New York Times Book Review*, *Slate*, and other publications. She is currently at work on a book about literature on the Holocaust.

MICHAEL HOFMANN was born in 1957 in Freiburg, Germany, and came to England in 1961. He has published four volumes of poems and won a Cholmondeley Award and the Geoffrey Faber Memorial Prize for poetry. His translations have won many awards, including the *Independent*'s Foreign Fiction Award, the International IMPAC Dublin Literary Award, and the PEN/Book-of-the-Month Club Translation Prize. His reviews and criticism are gathered in *Behind the Lines* (2001). He edited *The Faber Book of 20th Century German Poems* (2005), and his most recent work is the translation of the selected poems of Durs Grünbein, *Ashes for Breakfast* (2006).

ARTHUR LUBOW is a contributing writer to *The New York Times Magazine*, where he writes on cultural subjects. He is the author of *The Reporter Who Would Be King*, a biography of Richard Harding Davis, the American war correspondent and fin-de-siècle novelist.

TIM PARKS was born in Manchester, England, in 1954, grew up in London, and studied at Cambridge and Harvard. In 1981 he moved to Italy, where he has lived ever since. He has written eleven novels, including *Europa*, *Destiny*, *Rapids*, and *Cleaver*, as well as three nonfiction accounts of life in northern Italy (most recently, *A Season with Verona*), a collection of narrative essays, *Adultery and Other Diversions*, and a history of the Medici bank in fifteenth-century Florence, *Medici Money*. His many translations from the Italian include works by Alberto Moravia, Antonio Tabucchi, Italo Calvino, and Roberto Calasso. He lectures on literary translation in Milan.

MICHAEL SILVERBLATT is host and producer of public radio's premier literary talk show, *Bookworm*, which he created for KCRW-FM in Santa Monica, California, in 1989. Since that time, with the funding of the Lannan Foundation, *Bookworm* has achieved a national audience and reputation. Mr. Silverblatt has conducted nearly nine hundred interviews with many leading American and international writers. He was born in New York and educated at the State University in Buffalo and Johns Hopkins University. He moved to Los Angeles in the mid-1970s, where he worked in public relations and script development for the motion picture industry.

CHARLES SIMIC is a poet, essayist, and translator. He was born in Yugoslavia and immigrated to the United States in 1954. His first poems were published in 1959, when he was twenty-one. Since 1967 he has published twenty books of his own poetry (most recently *The Voice at 3:00 A.M.* and *My Noiseless Entourage*), seven books of essays, a memoir, and numerous translations of French, Serbian, Croatian, Macedonian, and Slovenian poetry for which he has received many literary awards, including the Pulitzer Prize, the Griffin Prize, and the MacArthur Fellowship. He is poetry editor of *The Paris Review* and professor emeritus of the University of New Hampshire, where he has taught since 1973.

ELEANOR WACHTEL is an award-winning writer and broadcaster. Based in Toronto, she is the host of CBC Radio's *Writers & Company* and *The Arts Tonight*. Three books of her interviews have been published: *Original Minds, Writers & Company*, and *More Writers & Company*.

SELECTED BIBLIOGRAPHY

IN ENGLISH
The Emigrants, New Directions, 1996
The Rings of Saturn, New Directions, 1998
Vertigo, New Directions, 1999
Austerlitz, Random House, 2001
After Nature, Random House, 2002
On the Natural History of Destruction, Random House, 2003
Campo Santo, Random House, 2005
Unrecounted, poems with lithographs by Jan Peter Tripp, New Directions, 2005

IN GERMAN
Nach der Natur: ein Elementargedicht, Franz Greno, 1988 (*After Nature*)
Schwindel. Gefuhle, Eichborn Verlag, 1990 (Vertigo)

Die Ausgewanderten, Eichborn Verlag, 1992 (*The Emigrants*)

Die Ringe des Saturn, Eine englische Wallfahrt, Eichborn Verlag, 1995 (*The Rings of Saturn*)

Luftkrieg und Literatur, Hanser Verlag, 1999 (*On the Natural History of Destruction*)

Austerlitz, Hanser Verlag, 2001

Campo Santo, Hanser Verlag, 2003

ABOUT THE EDITOR

LYNNE SHARON SCHWARTZ is the author of nineteen works of fiction, non-fiction, poetry, and memoir; most recently, the novel *Writing on the Wall*. She has been nominated for the National Book Award, the PEN/Hemingway Award for Best First Novel, and the PEN/Faulkner Award for Fiction, and she won the PEN Renato Poggioli Award for Translation in 1991.